SPITFIRE
ON
THE FAIRWAY

"The Answer to the Call."

SPITFIRE ON THE FAIRWAY

And Other Unexpected Hazards
of Golf in Wartime

Dale Concannon

AURUM PRESS
LONDON

For David Cronin, Tim Ward and John Sinnott.

With friends like you . . .

First published in Great Britain
2003 by Aurum Press Ltd
25 Bedford Avenue, London WC1B 3AT

PICTURE CREDITS
p. 17,134-135, the Phil Sheldon Golf Picture Library; 56, Hulton Archive;
127,129,136, Associated Press; 128, Corbis; 14, Mary Evans; 90 (HU 72691),
93 (HU 63829), 94 (A 14585), 99 (A 17137), 100 (A 4898), Imperial War Museum.
All other images from the Dale Concannon Golf History Collection
(c/o the Phil Sheldon Library).

Every effort has been made to trace the copyright holders of material
quoted in this book. If application is made in writing to the publisher,
any omissions will be included in future editions.

A catalogue record for this book is available from the British Library.

ISBN 1 85410 934 0

1 3 5 7 9 10 8 6 4 2
2003 2005 2007 2006 2004

Designed and typeset in 12 on 13½pt Dante by Peter Ward
Printed by MPG Books, Bodmin, Cornwall

CONTENTS

1944 *'It was just about here I hit that terrible drive to the seventeenth.'*

1945 *'It was just about here I grew that two-foot marrow.'*

Prince's Golf Club on the south coast of England was taken over by the army as a practice firing range. It was barely recognisable in wartime, and at least one former member had cause to be grateful that it was not ploughed up completely. Fighter ace Laddie Lucas, whose father had helped establish the club many years before, found himself in a Battle of Britain dogfight with his Spitfire running dangerously low on fuel and struggling to reach his base at Manston.

Spotting the Prince's clubhouse, he selected one of the fairways for an emergency landing. Overshooting slightly, he and his aircraft finished in the bushes somewhere behind the 9th green. A few days later, his old pal Henry Longhurst sent him a telegram that read: 'Bad driving. Poor show. I see you missed the fairway again.'

INTRODUCTION

THE GREAT WARTIME leader Winston Churchill once described golf as 'hitting a small ball into an even smaller hole with weapons ill-designed for the purpose'. He was probably right, yet it is overcoming this challenge that makes playing the game so rewarding. Perhaps that was the case in many of the stories detailed in this book. After all, what other reason can there be for playing golf in the middle of a war zone?

As a dedicated collector of golf books, I had long been frustrated by the apparent lack of information about the game during the war years. It was as though in the history of golf the years from 1914 to 1918 and from 1939 to 1945 never existed. But they did, and while major championships like the British Open and Ryder Cup were cancelled for the duration, golf continued to be played all over the world – often under the most bizarre of circumstances. As I began to research the untold story of wartime golf so many fascinating stories came to light. Many were bare snippets of information, tucked away in long-forgotten newspapers and magazines, but together they accumulated into an alternative history of the game I had never expected. I extended my search across the five centuries during which the game of golf had been in existence, and soon it became obvious the extent to which conflict of any kind impacts on the daily lives of ordinary people.

Thus it was with golf. From its earliest days right up to modern times, devotees of the sport have adapted their game to suit their circumstances, including wartime conditions. To paraphrase Churchill, they continued to golf on the beaches, in the fields and in the streets, and never surrendered, no matter how bad things got, or how impossible the conditions. Golfers will always golf. Perhaps that is what makes them such a special breed.

Dale Concannon

'A Very Nazi Lie'. On a course whose design has been modified the previous night by the Luftwaffe, a London golfer during World War II finds his 300-yard drive trapped by a new and very disagreeably-placed bunker in the middle of the first fairway.

PROLOGUE

ENGLAND DECLARED WAR at 11.00 a.m. on Sunday 3 September 3, 1939. An hour earlier, a foursome had teed off from the first at Royal St George's in Sandwich, Kent (scene of the 2003 British Open), including long-time member, Douglas Grant. If war was declared during their round, they asked the steward, would he mind raising the flag on top of the clubhouse? By the time they reached the tenth the flag was up. The party decided to continue. Grant was just at the top of his swing when an air-raid siren went off, causing him to shank his ball into a bunker. Red-faced with anger, he ordered his caddie to pick up the ball. 'If this damn war is going to spoil my golf,' he fulminated, 'I will pop over to Germany and have a word with Herr Hitler myself!'

For the second time in the twentieth century Britain, and golf, were at war. But the game of golf was going to fight on the links, on the fairways and on the greens: it was not about to let the threat of mere aerial bombardment or invasion interrupt the civilised battle between ball and hole. 'Now that National Service has demanded the services of most people,' a correspondent wrote to *Golf Monthly* in October 1939, 'caddies are very scarce on the golf courses. On the Continent, girls have always carried golf clubs, presumably because they wanted to, and if some of us make our bags a little lighter, I think we might encourage them to do the same here.'

A year after Mr Grant's shanked shot at Sandwich, September 9th 1940, at the height of the Battle of Britain, James Sheridan, caddie master at Sunningdale, decided to help out by mowing the 18th green on the Old Course. He had covered just over half of it when a huge explosion came from over the road on the ladies' course. Another exploded just 200 yards away down the fairway, and Mr Sheridan realised the bombs were landing in a line. Diving for cover, he threw himself into the bunker on the right hand side of the green. As he

3

did so, another bomb fell short of the green to the left. In the next three minutes 100 bombs rained down on the golf course and surrounding area. It seemed some German bombers had been attacked by Spitfires and had immediately ditched their bombs for a speedy escape. With the clubhouse barely touched, the indomitable Sheridan climbed out of his green-side bunker, dusted himself down and finished off the green.

Indeed, as the war dragged on, the threat of aerial bombardment on a golf course remained ever-present, even when there were no German bombers overhead. The following year, the issue of *Golf Monthly* for March 1941 reported that at a golf course in the London area a couple of delayed-action bombs had been found. A bomb-disposal squad arrived to deal with them, and the sergeant asked the local professional to show him where they were. As they were walking up the fairway, the sergeant, after several nervous glances over his shoulder, asked, 'Is there any golf played here now?'

'Oh, yes, but not a lot,' replied the pro.

'Well, that's all right,' said the sergeant. 'I just wanted to know. I don't want to get a smack in the back of the neck with a golf ball – that's blasted dangerous!'

Not that danger was anything new to devotees of the Royal and Ancient Game.

For the past five centuries or more, warfare had had a regular habit of intruding into this hitherto tranquil sport.

CHAPTER I

Some Early Skirmishes
1450 to 1750

A s FAR BACK AS 1457, King James II of Scotland declared war on golf. Too many of his subjects, it seemed, preferred to spend their time on the links rather than fine-tune their archery skills. With the English threatening invasion from the south, and previous warnings having gone unheeded, radical action had to be taken. Regular archery practice was now deemed vital to the defence of the realm, and so a decree went out in every town and village. 'Golf,' it proclaimed, was to 'be utterly cryit doune and nocht be usit.'

But the Scots are a stubborn breed. Despite a punitive fine of two pennies levied on any male who failed to attend his local archery range and *'schutte six schottes at the least'* they refused to give up their favourite pastime. In 1471 and 1491 the ban was renewed, but still failed to eradicate this *'unproffitable sport'*. Subsequent Scottish kings finally accepted the inevitable and took up the game themselves.

After James IV signed the Treaty of Glasgow with Henry VII of England in 1502, a period of relative calm ensued. The Scottish monarch was invited by his nobles to try the game of golf for himself. At first he refused point blank, but then he began hitting a few shots at Holyrood House in Edinburgh. Before the year was out he had purchased his first set of clubs from a longbow maker in Perth. The golf bug had struck! February 1503 was spent playing golf and hunting, and the royal accounts reveal a 'hidden' payment of three French

At Leith in Scotland in 1641, King Charles I receives the news that civil war has broken out in Ireland and has to abandon his round of golf to depart post-haste for Holyrood and London.

crowns to the Earl of Bothwell – not the last time the public purse would be called upon to pay the king's golfing debts. But it was war that brought to an end James IV's promise as a champion golfer – a career as short-lived as his treaty with England. In 1513 he was killed at Flodden. It was James IV's association with golf that earned it the title of 'Royal and Ancient Game' but, interestingly, he never did lift that early decree outlawing golf.

The sport was now played throughout Scotland and golf and war were to come together again there just over a century later. During the battle of Kirkwall Castle in 1614 the Earl of Caithness – obviously a keen player away from his military duties – observed how 'the canon balls of the besiegers were broken like golf balls and cloven in two halves.' Historians now conclude from the earl's description that the first balls were made from wood rather than the leather-covered feathery balls so popular in the early 1800s. Then again, he may just have been a chronic 'topper' of the ball.

Another tragic figure from golf's distant past is King Charles I of England. Grandson to the unfortunate James IV, he is known to have been playing golf on Leith Links in 1641 when news of the Irish rebellion was brought to him. A keen if headstrong player, he is also reported to have played at Newcastle-upon-Tyne five years later while being held captive by the Scots.

After the demise of the Stuart line in 1714, royal golfers were less in evidence until Bonnie Prince Charlie, whose obvious passion for the game matched his illustrious ancestors'. Whether he brought his clubs over from France in 1745 during his abortive attempt to seize the English throne is unknown, but he finished his days in exile playing solitary rounds in the Borghese Gardens in Rome. Even the Young Pretender, however, could not have envisaged the crisis that golf would face over the coming century.

CLASSIFIED ADVERT
Printed in *The Times*: April 1917:

GOLF: Officer on leave in South West London wishes morning lessons from professional. Currently belongs to no club. Apply Box no. 2126.

ROYAL NAVY OFFICER on leave wants as golfing companion another officer, handicap about 8, for fortnightly golf in north Devon. Apply Box no. 3621.

CHAPTER II

When Golf Nearly Died
1751 to 1898

IMAGINE A WORLD without golf.

A grey world with no possibility of a 300-yard drive or
match-winning putt to thrill the senses. A world where the
names of Jack Nicklaus and Tiger Woods meant nothing,
where picturesque golf courses remained farmers' fields or
sandy wastelands. Too frightening to contemplate? During the
nineteenth century, however, we came close to losing our
favourite sport forever.

Most histories of golf appear to show a steady increase in
popularity from the mid-1700s right up to the modern day. A
closer look, however, reveals a different story – that, within a
few years of the first Scottish golf clubs being formed, the
game had fallen into apparently terminal decline, along with
long forgotten pastimes like cambuc and stool-ball. Even
Scotland, the 'Home of Golf', had turned its back on the
game, with many of its great links – including St Andrews –
sold off for farmland and under imminent danger of being
ploughed up. By 1835, caddies stood idle on the links while
skilled club and feathery ball makers had long since lost their
livelihoods through lack of custom. Having been played for
over four hundred years, the game of golf was in imminent
danger of dying out forever.

How did this crisis arise? Even after Bonnie Prince
Charlie's disastrous foray into England there had been little
sign of the trouble to come. In the decades that followed golf

8

was adopted by the middle and upper classes of Scottish society despite their having to share the links with the red-coated English officers who also found it a pleasant and healthy way to pass the time. In 1744 the Honourable Company of Edinburgh Golfers formed the first official golf club and, despite having its first captain, John Rattray, arrested after the Battle of Culloden for tending the Scottish wounded, was soon flourishing. Thirteen basic rules were formulated by which the game could be played, and courses like Musselburgh and Bruntsfield became crowded with eager converts, the only restriction being that no one should play on the Sabbath.

But after 14 July 1789 all that was to change, and the catalyst was civil war – though this time not in Britain. Ignited by the storming of the Bastille in Paris, the French Revolution lit a flame across Europe. The lower classes had risen up against their aristocratic masters and threatened the fundamental hierarchy of British society. In Edinburgh, English troops opened fire on a crowd chanting pro-Napoleonic slogans. By the later years of the 18th century lower-class

HOW TO EXPOSE A SPY IN THE CLUBHOUSE:

These persons are very cunning and are liable to frequent any places where men and women get together to talk, like a golf club. If you see a dark or bearded stranger your midst, it is your duty as a citizen to discover his identity. Stamp smartly on his toe or knock his drink (if he has one) carefully, where it will cause him most inconvenience. If he swears at you in a foreign tongue, you may congratulate yourself on having accomplished a smart performance. Rapid thinking of this sort will take you quickly into the Secret Service. Again, always beware of those exotic blondes who offer you champagne from their bedroom slippers. That sort of thing just spells 'secret agent.'

Advice from the Editor of *Golf Monthly*, September 1939

resentment – fuelled by spiralling prices for bread and ale – of anyone considered upper-class included anyone who played golf! Known by the red hunting jackets they wore on the links, members of elite golf societies like the Honourable Company or Society of St Andrews Golfers were often abused as they left their carriages. With major cities like Edinburgh and Glasgow becoming increasingly tense, the 'Gentleman Golfers' began to avoid the links, fearing in some cases for their lives. Courses like Leith and Bruntsfield quickly fell into disrepair, their greens soon overgrown. Local hostelries who reserved rooms for club meetings and after-match celebrations struggled to survive and, though a smattering of local golfers still ventured out with a club and a ball, it was not enough to maintain those caddies and club makers who relied on the sport just to eat.

Away from the big cities the situation was little better. Food was short and while sandy links-land was totally unsuitable for growing much-needed basics like wheat and potatoes, there was pressure to make better use of the land. In 1797, the town council at St Andrews was forced to sell the ancient links on which golf had been played for centuries. The new owner established a large-scale rabbit-breeding business on the land previously used for golf, with new burrows appearing on greens and tees almost every day. Fortunately the few remaining members of the Society of St Andrews Golfers took their case all the way to the House of Lords, where they managed to establish the ancient right of 'usage' over ownership and the farmer and his rabbits were unceremoniously thrown off. (But not before an aged St Andrews caddie was brought to London to testify that golf had indeed been played on the Old Course in the decades prior to the dispute!)

With golf now considered a relic of the past, and the Industrial Revolution causing towns and cities across Scotland to grow at an alarming rate, house builders took full advantage of the common land on which the game was played. On the outskirts of Edinburgh both Leith and Bruntsfield Links

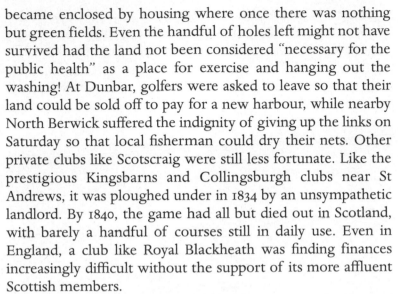

became enclosed by housing where once there was nothing but green fields. Even the handful of holes left might not have survived had the land not been considered "necessary for the public health" as a place for exercise and hanging out the washing! At Dunbar, golfers were asked to leave so that their land could be sold off to pay for a new harbour, while nearby North Berwick suffered the indignity of giving up the links on Saturday so that local fisherman could dry their nets. Other private clubs like Scotscraig were still less fortunate. Like the prestigious Kingsbarns and Collingsburgh clubs near St Andrews, it was ploughed under in 1834 by an unsympathetic landlord. By 1840, the game had all but died out in Scotland, with barely a handful of courses still in daily use. Even in England, a club like Royal Blackheath was finding finances increasingly difficult without the support of its more affluent Scottish members.

How the game of golf pulled itself back from the brink of extinction has always been a matter for debate, but essentially the social and industrial revolutions that threatened its very survival ultimately became its saviours. Production of the cheaper gutta-percha ball from 1848 made a round of golf much cheaper, and the rapid expansion of the railways put a sleepy university town like St Andrews within easy reach of Edinburgh and Glasgow. Over the next fifty years the same prosperity came to other resort towns like Troon, North Berwick, Carnoustie, Cruden Bay and Prestwick (which in 1860 hosted the very first British Open Championship).

Countless hotels sprang up in the late 1890s to satisfy the demand for a round of golf as an essential part of the 'holiday experience' at English seaside resorts, too, like Blackpool and

Two-times United States Amateur winner, Robert A. Gardner, was the first well-known golfer to achieve a commissioned rank in World War I. Champion in 1909 and 1915, the Chicago-born golfer became a first lieutenant in the 338th Field Artillery based at Camp Dodge, Iowa.

Southport. Where in 1851 there were just 24 Golf Clubs in the whole of Great Britain, less than half a century later there were 1,276. The game had not only survived but prospered.

By the end of the century, however, some of the game's enthusiastic converts were being caught up in a new war far away from home.

In 1915, the British attempted to end the deadlock of trench warfare in France by forcing a passage through the Dardanelles and forcing Turkey out of the war. This poorly conceived plan ended in failure and humiliation, perhaps best revealed by the attitude of some of the officer corps. Within days of arriving, a rough 9-hole golf course was laid out within sight of the Gallipoli Peninsula. With the enemy looking on incredulously, young dispatch carriers were drafted in as caddies while the officers played competitions among themselves. Describing the fun, Lieutenant Jenkins wrote: 'The best round ever was 42. The going was heavy with much sand, while in other areas there were some very unnatural bunkers of practice trenches and dugouts. The greens were so bad that there was no chance of holing out until the player had manoeuvred his ball within what was called "a leather" (grip) of the hole…'

CHAPTER III

The Boer War
A High Cost to Pay: 1899 to 1902

T HE BOER WAR, fought in far-off South Africa, had little effect on day-to-day life in Britain. Yet the cost to golf was truly significant in terms of those killed because among the fallen was Frederick Guthrie Tait. A two-time British Amateur champion and the most highly regarded golfer of his generation, 'F.G' began his soldiering in the Royal Ulster Rifles

in 1892 before transferring to a regiment more in keeping with his Scottish roots, the Black Watch. Leading amateur in the British Open in 1894, 1896 and 1899 he won the Hampshire Amateur Championship in 1894 with borrowed clubs while stationed at nearby Aldershot. He was shot through the heart at Koodoos-burg Drift near Magersfontein on 7 February 1900 during a reconnaissance mission and was buried on the banks of the nearby Riet River. News of his tragic death was followed by a day of mourning in St Andrews.

Two-time British Amateur champion Frederick Tait in his Black Watch uniform.

John Ball, double British Open and Amateur champion in 1890, and later heroic Boer War horseman.

Another legendary amateur who served in the Boer War was Tait's greatest rival from the unpaid ranks, John Ball Jr, a double British Open and Amateur winner in 1890. They met in the final of the Amateur Championship in 1899 where Ball found himself 5-down before coming back to win on the 37th hole.

Ball was an excellent horseman and crack shot, and his popularity was such that members at Royal Liverpool, Lytham and Leosowe collected enough money to buy him a 'fine charger, Mauser pistol and field glasses'. Having undergone training at Wrexham and Aldershot, he paid a final visit to Hoylake prior to leaving for South Africa in February 1900. The local newspaper proclaimed 'all honour to those who prefer the storming of the kopje to the bunker,' and Trooper Ball of the Denbigh Yeomanry was met by a large crowd at the railway station who cheered 'themselves hoarse' as he departed.

Involved in some of the most violent skirmishes of the entire campaign, Ball had his beloved charger shot from underneath him in September and was forced to escape on foot 'with the Boers sending a shower of bullets after him'. Barely recovered from the leg injury he sustained, he was back in action two months later, saving a fellow soldier who became trapped under the weight of his own horse. Ball was a shy and unassuming individual, so it was left to his colleague, Trooper Hinde, to describe his brave act in a letter:

In the gallop from the breakwater one man's horse came
down and John Ball immediately pulled up and went to his
assistance, getting the horse up from the poor beggar's legs
– all of this under heavy cross fire . . . Ball is too modest to
speak about himself in any such connection and won't
have his name in the papers if he can possibly help it . . .

His homecoming to Hoylake in July 1901 was greeted with
scenes as joyful as those at his departure 18 months earlier,
with hundreds of well-wishers there to greet him. Having
suffered a family bereavement a week earlier, he and his sister
slipped quietly away from the throng. Ball returned to
tournament golf a short time later.

Two lesser-known golfing victims of the Boer War were
Major Tawse of St Andrews and Webster Prentice, former South
African golf champion. Blinded in South Africa and treated at
the same field hospital as Ball in Harrisburg, Tawse returned to
Scotland determined to carry on playing golf in spite of his
terrible injury. He would kneel down before each shot and touch
the ball to ascertain his lie, and take up his stance. His caddie
would then ring a small hand bell to show him the direction to
hit. Prentice's claim to fame was leaving £60 to the South African
Golf Union when he was killed at the battle of Hooge. The first
legacy of its kind, it was intended 'for the encouragement of the
game among the youth of South Africa'.

Former US Open champion Willie Smith was killed at Mexico City Golf
Club when it was shelled during the Revolution in 1915.

In 1942 a golfer playing at Killermount Golf Club near Glasgow sliced his
approach into a towering beech tree. The tree keeled over and the golfer
claimed this was due to the force of his shot. On closer inspection, however,
it was found that a bomb had fallen close by the night before.

CHAPTER IV

Battle of the Sexes
Golf and the Suffragettes:
1903 to 1913

GOLF HAS LONG PROVED a battleground for women. Treated as second-class citizens in a male-dominated sport, they have struggled to gain equality. Even in these so-called enlightened times some of the most famous golf clubs in the world, including a number of major venues, steadfastly refuse to accept women members; and even those that accept them often restrict the times they can play, in accordance with the wishes of the male members. In the words of one former US Open women's champion: 'As long as golf is run by men for men, it's a battle of the sexes which will probably go on as long as the game is played . . .'

The struggle for equal rights began well over a century ago. Golf was considered an unsuitable pastime for women, the main complaint centring on the actual physical activity. In the Victorian era physical exertion of any kind was closely associated with the lower classes and the very thought that a cultured young lady might raise a club above her head was considered quite shocking. As Lord Wellwood commented in 1890, 'The postures and gestures requisite for a full swing are not particularly graceful when the player is clad in female dress' – and indeed, playing golf in a whalebone corset cannot have been easy. But the mere thought of a woman's presence on the links proved too much of an annoyance for some men. Earlier, in 1867, *Cornhill Magazine* had reported the comments

Mary, Queen of Scots essays the first shot in golf's battle of the sexes.

of one irate male golfer who found his playing partner had brought his wife and sister-in-law along for company. 'The links are not the place for women,' he complained. 'They talk incessantly, never stand still and even if they do, the wind won't allow their dresses to stand still!'

Even in Scotland, where golf was a game played by everyone from the Laird to the local shopkeeper, most women golfers had to content themselves with an occasional putt when no one was looking. And as early as 1565, Mary, Queen of Scots's supposed levity in playing golf on Seton fields barely days after the murder of her husband Lord Darnley was given as evidence in her subsequent trial. It helped discredit her in the eyes of the English court and to provide sufficient reason for Queen Elizabeth I to have her executed.

It would be another 300 years before women golfers fired – or at least played – the first shot in this battle of the sexes. Unable to join their husbands on the links, a small group of women began playing golf on waste ground near the town

railway station at St. Andrews in 1860. Led by Mrs Robert
Boothby, wife of a prominent member of the R&A, they
would sneak onto a rough course laid out by local caddies. But
the terrible sight of women hitting golf balls brought a tidal
wave of male condemnation. Husbands were summoned into
the club to explain the behaviour of their spouses, and the
women were ordered to turn in their clubs with immediate
effect.

To her credit, the formidable Mrs Boothby never gave up
on the idea of playing golf. A constant thorn in the side of the
R&A, in 1866 she was instrumental in securing a small strip of
land adjacent to the Old Course, with just enough room for an
18-hole putting course. A year later she formed the St Andrews
Ladies' Golf Club, with herself as president. Still in existence
today, it proved an important stepping stone in the acceptance
of woman golfers.

After some initial resistance, the men could not help but
be impressed with the skill exhibited by these women. Regular
competitions were held over the 'Himalayas' putting course,
and author Robert Clark wrote in 1875 of how 'the skill of the
fair competitors is by no means to be despised. On their own
ground, the best of them would be backed freely against the
cracks of the R&A.'

Despite their best efforts, there was still no question of
women being allowed to play with their husbands on the Old
Course, or on any other course in Scotland for that matter.
But having established an important toehold, women golfers
were not easily put off. By 1893, there were enough of them in
England and Scotland to form the Ladies' Golf Union, creat-
ing a framework by which women's championships could be
formally sanctioned. The progress from golfing outcasts to
respected female golfers had been little short of meteoric.

The first British Ladies' Championship, held at Royal
Lytham in 1893, was another major turning point for the
women's game. It was won by Lady Margaret Scott, who
captured the public's imagination, personifying the game for

many people with her youthful vigour and free-flowing swing. Her three wins in the event made golf hugely fashionable among the upper classes, especially in England. Attractive and personable, she became something of a celebrity in London society, *Golf Illustrated* describing her game as 'graceful, yet powerful'.

After her departure in the late 1890s, the women's game looked for a new heroine. Fitting the bill, a young girl from Silloth in Cumbria named Cecilia Leitch took centre stage in 1910 when she challenged the former British Open and Amateur champion Harold Hilton in a 72-hole match over Sunningdale and Walton Heath. The main purpose of the match, sponsored by *The Ladies' Field* magazine, was to promote women's golf; and it certainly captured the public's imagination. This was a time when women's issues were at the forefront of political debate, and thousands of curious spectators turned up at both venues to see whether the 19-year-old girl could topple the 41-year-old golfing legend. With no ladies' tees to speak of, it was agreed that Leitch should play off the same tees as Hilton! At a major disadvantage, she was compensated for her lack of distance by receiving one stroke every second hole, but was not expected to run Hilton even close. She later described the build-up to the match and its eventual outcome:

> The 'test' in which Mr. Hilton and I met was one of 72 holes – 36 at Walton Heath, 36 at Sunningdale – on October 11 and 13, 1910. For weeks before, the match was widely discussed, opinions greatly differing as to the probable result . . . Perhaps I was given some confidence by the wise and encouraging advice of that wonderful judge of form, James Braid, who during a friendly round at Walton Health told me just to play my own game and I would come through . . . So unique a match was likely to attract a following, but I shall never forget my surprise when I arrived at the Clubhouse at Walton Heath to find a crowd

Harold Hilton and Cecilia Leitch: a 72-hole showdown at Sunningdale and Walton Heath.

of about 3,000 spectators, one of the biggest crowds ever seen on a Southern course. At times it was hard to find room to swing a club, so eager was the crowd to see every stroke, and on one occasion Mr. Hilton was not allowed to finish his follow through! The chief thing that I recollect

about the first half of the match is that I seldom saw my
opponent play a shot through the green. It was only after
the crowd had formed a circle around the green that I was
given an opportunity to watch Mr. Hilton. We both struck
a patch of somewhat indifferent play during the first 36
holes and both slipped a number of chances, but on the
other hand we occasionally did something brilliant . . .
The result of the first day's play was a lead of 1 hole for
my opponent.

The considerate organisers of the match allowed us a
day's rest before commencing the second half of the match.
At Walton Heath we had a perfect day; at Sunningdale the
weather conditions could not have been worse – a gale of
wind and drenching rain . . . I remember little about the
third round except that we were soaked to the skin before
we reached the first green, and that I was 4 down with 18
holes to play.

Consider this scenario: a young woman in a man's game,
pitted against a seasoned veteran, in driving rain, 4 down with
one round left. How many people today could even walk 36
holes a day, let alone do it in a rainstorm?

In the afternoon a win in 4 at the 1st hole [not a stroke
hole] slightly improved my position, but the next two holes
went to my opponent, and I felt that any chance of success
I had ever possessed had now finally vanished. Five down
and fifteen to play with 8 strokes to come! The only thing
that now interested me was to try to make my defeat as
light as possible. On the 4th green Mr. Hilton missed a
comparatively short putt, which allowed me to win back a
hole with the help of the stroke allowance. In a 72-holes
match the pendulum swings first one way and then the
other, but little did I think as I took the honour on the fifth
tee of the fourth round that the time had come for it to
take a decided swing in my favour. From that point I lost

*only 1 hole, and eventually won on the 71st green by 2 up
and 1 to play.*

Women having campaigned unsuccessfully for the vote
since 1905, the result received a great deal of publicity and was
acclaimed by the Women's Movement as a blow against male
domination. All Cecilia Leitch would say was 'how much the
match had increased the interest taken in ladies' golf.'

She was right. In 1911, a silent movie titled *The Suffragette's
Downfall* was released: the plot concerns two women, both
ardent suffragettes, who go off to play golf while their
husbands take care of the children and do the shopping! This
scenario bore little resemblance to real-life women golfers in
Britain. The film was banned from theatres in London on the
grounds that it was 'inflammatory'.

With golf increasingly seen as a bastion of male privilege
by the Women's Social and Political Union (WSPU) and their
charismatic leader, Emmeline Pankhurst, more forceful action
was called for by *The Suffragette* in February 1913. Edited by
Emmeline's sister Christabel, the publication praised those
women who dug up greens in the dead of night or poured
weedkiller over them, under the provocative headline 'The
Tearing of the Greens':

> *Some people say the suffragettes have acted very unwisely
> in destroying golf greens because this has made golfers very
> angry. Yet what is there to fear from their anger? What
> have (male) golfers ever done for Suffrage cause, and what
> will they ever do, if they are left to play their game in
> peace? Some golfers are members of the Liberal
> Government and they have done the Women's Cause a very
> great injury. The others have never done it any good. The
> editor of* Golfing *says that golfers are usually not very
> deep politicians. Perhaps they will be now that the
> Suffragettes have taught them the very close connection
> with golf and politics. Of course they are very angry with*

DON'T BE SURPRISED IF IT'S YOUR WIFE WHO DOCTORS THE GREENS!

the Suffragettes but that is much better than their former
state of indifference… To all golfers we say: Use the power
and influence which you as a citizen possess to get justice
for woman and protection for your greens! You are
hopelessly stymied and the only way to negotiate is to do
what we advise.

The crisis was reaching boiling point, with courses at West Essex, Raynes Park, Mid-Surrey and Swinley Forest all attacked within a month. At Woking Golf Club in March 1913, vitriol was used to mark out the words 'VOTES BEFORE SPORT' and 'NO VOTES, NO GOLF.' An appeal was made to members of golf clubs in the Surrey area to pressurise 'troublesome' wives or daughters into desisting from such reckless action. It obviously had little effect: at Sandwich in August, a group of suffragettes ambushed Winston Churchill on his way back from a round of golf. Surrounding his car with their bicycles, they attempted to involve him in a debate before he finally managed to drive away. Frustrated at his lack of interest, a local newspaper then reported how holes had

been scooped out of two of the greens at Royal St George's and leaflets inserted bearing the slogan 'VOTES FOR WOMEN'.

Questions were asked in the Houses of Parliament – especially after former prime minister David Lloyd George was 'debagged' while playing golf at Walton Heath. The more militant the suffragettes grew, the more entrenched the Government became. More bombs were planted; peaceful protest turned into riots, with a number of buildings torched, including golf clubhouses, cricket pavilions and racecourse grandstands. It was the worst kind of stalemate and would have continued unresolved had it not been for the onset of war. Suspending all militant action from April 1914, Pankhurst declared that women had a 'higher loyalty to the country' and would take up the issue after the conflict had been 'successfully concluded'.

In the end, many of the issues resolved themselves. By taking up jobs in munitions factories, farms and other hitherto 'male-only' jobs, women gained a new position in society.

Golfing hazards encountered by Lloyd George at Walton Heath ranged from this ball plugged in a bunker to being debagged by the suffragettes.

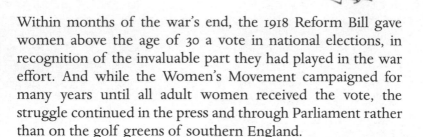

Within months of the war's end, the 1918 Reform Bill gave women above the age of 30 a vote in national elections, in recognition of the invaluable part they had played in the war effort. And while the Women's Movement campaigned for many years until all adult women received the vote, the struggle continued in the press and through Parliament rather than on the golf greens of southern England.

Tregenna Castle in Cornwall played host to many important guests before World War II, including Von Ribbentrop, German Ambassador to Great Britain. It was a widely held belief that St Ives would never be bombed, because Hitler had promised Tregenna to Herr Von Ribbentrop as a personal residence after Germany had conquered Britain.

At the end of every Red Cross exhibition match during World War I, a charity auction was held where various items would be sold off to raise funds. Mostly these would be eggs, butter and fruit, but among the most unusual items offered for sale at Sunningdale on October 1917 were 'four pieces of Zeppelin skin brought down in Suffolk'. They fetched £8, which paled in comparison with the £20 paid for a signed photograph of Lord Kitchener but at least outstripped the meagre £2 offered for a similar photo of the Kaiser!

Emblem here of rage—amaze—
Poor deluded caddie says:
"Hello, Bill, we're bunkered."

CHIPS OF THE OLD BLOCK.

CHAPTER V

World War I
The British Empire Strikes Back:
1914 to 1918

THE 'GREAT WAR' began as a regional conflict between Austria-Hungary and Serbia after the assassination of Archduke Francis Ferdinand in Sarajevo on 28 June 1914, and quickly escalated into a global conflict involving 32 nations, 12 million deaths and an economic cost running into billions. Germany declared war on France on 3 August and began marching on Paris from the north via Belgium. The violation of Belgium's official neutrality prompted Britain to declare war on Germany on 4 August.

With the fate of Europe now hanging in the balance, Austria-Hungary, Bulgaria and Turkey joined a well-armed Germany in a menacing coalition against the 'allied' nations of Britain, France, Italy and eventually the United States. The two great armies met near the River Somme in Northern France in September 1914 and barely moved 500 yards either way during four years of bloody stalemate. A 600-mile front stretched from the North Sea down to Switzerland in the south. It seemed indeed 'the war to end all wars'.

Back in Britain, there was little sign of the nightmare to come as countless thousands of young men, whipped up by patriotic fervour, signed up to fight the 'Hun' from September 1914 onward. The claim that it would all 'be over by Christmas' was soon exposed as over-optimistic, as news from the front became increasingly bleak. The area between the two

implacable enemies – small enough for them to hear each other singing Christmas carols in December 1914 – became known as 'no-man's-land'. During battle machine-gunners swept across the area with murderous accuracy, with snipers to finish off the survivors. The water-filled, rat-infested trenches were barely deep enough to offer shelter from the constant barrage of 'whizz-bang' shells, and in the early part of the war more soldiers died from frostbite, trench foot and diarrhoea than from enemy fire.

Politically Britain was in turmoil. Prime Minister Herbert Asquith struggled hard to control factions within his own government who argued that Britain should not have become involved in the first place. When the war appeared to be going badly in 1915, he drafted in David Lloyd George to become his Minister of Munitions. The coalition government quickly began to undermine Asquith's leadership in favour of the charismatic Welshman. Having agreed to collaborate with the opposition Conservative Party, Lloyd George replaced Asquith as Prime Minister in December 1916 and would be in overall charge of the war effort until the Armistice was signed in 1918.

Sport came a distant second behind the more pressing economic issues of the time, and while golf was still popular with the moneyed classes, it would suffer more than most other sports as the dark clouds of war descended. By the time war was declared memberships were already down and fewer golf courses were being built than at any time over the previous two decades.

Even the crowds at the Open Championship seemed smaller, despite the continued presence of those legends of the game, Harry Vardon, James Braid and J.H. Taylor. Not even nostalgic Open victories for Taylor in 1913 and Vardon in 1914 had succeeded in capturing the public imagination, and America was the new breeding ground for top-class golfers. British golf wanted new stars to cheer on, and apart from big-hitting professionals like George Duncan and Abe Mitchell, the cupboard was embarrassingly bare. *The Times* worsened the

Harry Vardon and James Braid in a World War I exhibition match.

situation with a withering attack in July 1914 describing the 'decadent effect the game produced on the youth of the country, the selfishness it engendered and the meanness of spirit'.

It was left to *Golf Monthly* editor Harold Hilton to bang the drum for the British golfer, along with a little anti-German propaganda:

> *The War hangs like a deathly pall over the land of golf. On the eastern seaboard of Britain the peaceful resorts are largely in the hands of the military authorities, vast entrenchments have been constructed and the adjacent ground turned into tented fields. It is no purpose of ours to discuss the cause or significance of the terrible campaign. Those of us who have travelled in Germany have had graven into the mind, the all-pervading worship of the military spirit, the joy of the people of the Fatherland in the rattle of the scabbard and the clank of the soldier's step . . .*

*The golfers of the Kingdom have made a noble
response in the hour of the Empire's distress. Everywhere,
competitions likely to attract the youth of the country were
abandoned, clubhouses made ready for the suitable reception
of the wounded, accompanied by guarantees to fit them up
with all medical appliances and provide with medical and
nursing skill should they be required. We have no desire to
draw comparisons at such a moment, but no sport can
excel the answer which golf has made in the hour of
national need . . . At the rumble of the drum, the best of
our manhood in the golf clubs throughout the Kingdom
rallied around the old flag and at the moment some of the
finest golfers in the land are answering the bugle call on the
bloody fields of France and Belgium.*

The duration and outcome of the war formed an endless
subject for clubhouse conversation in the second half of
1914. In October, 50 golf clubs in the London area passed a
resolution demanding that every German and Austrian-born
member 'should cease to frequent their respective clubs for
the duration of the war and those not naturalised should
be immediately expelled'. This was typical of the hard-line
attitude of many British subjects – the swiftness of the
German assault on France had shocked everyone. But according to *Golf Monthly* magazine the final outcome of the war
was never in doubt because the Germans were not golfers:

*The fortune of war will vary, the pendulum will swing but
the final issue can never be in doubt. The Germans have
never shown themselves the least inclined for golf, and at
Berlin and Frankfurt, where the game has got some substantial hold, its popularity is not with the Deutsch, but with
the British population, very numerous in both cities . . .
Right and justice must triumph and even though the
legions of the mad war dog have gained an early advantage, the advantage must be temporary, and the day will*

come when the tide of battle shall roll back across the
French frontiers, over Belgium and into the Fatherland.

Promoting the ideal that Britain was the home of fair play, many schemes sprang up to assist less fortunate members of society, including caddies. It was suggested that well-heeled golfers 'should continue to employ their caddies and not deprive them of their daily bread', but this brought howls of complaint from those who thought that caddies should be enlisting like everyone else. As Harold Hilton wrote in his *Golf Monthly* editorial of September 1914:

I should say that no caddie between the ages of 19 and 35 be
given a single job or the slightest encouragement to be about
the links. Every one of these men, if they are physically fit,
ought to be in the firing line. They are accustomed to the
open-air life, to roughing it, and with their keen eyesight
and general hardiness every man jack of them at this
present moment should be wearing the King's uniform. My
best advice to golf clubs is to assist these young fellows to
get to the nearest recruiting station, and refuse to permit
them to hang about the caddie master's box.

The editor then outlines the reason why Germany cannot win the war and why good golfers make even better soldiers:

The implements of the game have been thrown aside and the
men who wielded them, we venture to say, by their clean
lives, the strength which they acquired in playing their quiet
and secluded pastime, the sociability in their nature rooted
in them by pleasant intercourse with their fellow men, will
make them as soldiers on the battlefield or as comrades on
the hard ground... the very best material in our fighting line.

Propaganda was a useful tool in 1914 but failed to mask the inherent problems British golf faced in time of war. *Golf*

HOW TO MAKE GOLF POSSIBLE IN WAR-TIME.
A FEW SUGGESTIONS FOR EASING THE PLAYER'S CONSCIENCE.

THE HOGGED MOUSTACHE.

SALUTING A PLUS-MAN.

A FOURSOME "FALLING-IN."

NO MORE OF THESE GRACEFUL FINISHES. HAVING STRUCK THE BALL, THE PLAYER RETURNS SMARTLY TO THE "ORDER."

THE MID-DAY HALT.

SENDING THE "WILL-YOU-COME-THROUGH" SIGNAL.

NO QUARTER GIVEN.

"AT EASE."

Illustrated suggested that each Golf Club in Britain raise at least £100 towards the war effort, but for many even this amount was hard to find. With competitions cancelled for the foreseeable future, the revenue so vital to the survival of many clubs was severely curtailed. Golfers were enlisting in ever-greater numbers and increasingly taking the cheaper option of clubhouse privileges rather than paying full membership fees. In London especially, a lack of income proved fatal: Honor Oak Golf Club, Park Royal and West Drayton all failed to survive the war. (Ravenscliffe, the first club in Yorkshire to allow Sunday golf, was also wound up in 1916.)

The wholesale abandonment of fixtures in the second half of 1914 – both professional and amateur – meant that golf had effectively gone into hibernation with no sign of when it would return. The Welsh Amateur Championship was among the first to be cancelled, along with the prestigious £400 *News of the World* tournament. Then came news that the much anticipated match between English and Scottish professionals at Royal Mid-Surrey near London had also been cancelled.

In 1915, the first thing British golfers noticed was the rising cost of golf balls. With industry geared to the war effort, the manufacture of sporting goods understandably took second place to that of military hardware while commodities like rubber were diverted to the production of tyres, hoses, belts, moulding and gaskets. As the conflict continued unabated, the five-minute rule for finding lost balls was widely flouted as golfers recognised the high cost of losing one in the rough. Repainted balls became commonplace as old gutties, popular twenty years earlier, were dusted off and played with. Theft was also a growing problem. At South Staffordshire, gangs of local boys invaded the course in search of lost balls which would then be offered for sale back to the members. Then, as the shortage became even more acute, a network of criminals began paying caddies to pilfer the odd ball or two. 'I had a personal experience of a loafer offering me half a dozen balls,' reported one irate reader in *Golf Illustrated*. 'It was on a busy road near a first class London club. His pockets were full of them and as most golfers are careless about the number they own, the amount that can be stolen is quite staggering.'

A lack of playable balls was not the only difficulty golfers endured during the early years of the war. With patriotic fer-

*First Golfer (to friend who has come
from a distance to play with him).*
'BUT, MY DEAR CHAP,
WHERE ARE YOUR CLUBS?'

Second Golfer. 'HUSH! NOT A WORD!
I'VE GOT 'EM DISGUISED IN HERE!'

vour at its zenith those who could not resist playing their favourite game faced public condemnation every time they stepped onto the links. It was widely accepted that any member home on leave could play free of charge, but those in so-called 'reserved' occupations, such as food suppliers or factory owners, often faced the gauntlet of local opinion. In November 1915, *Golf Monthly* reported how one professional would not take his clubs openly across London to give a lesson but had them packed in a box and sent by messenger. It was the same in Dublin, as the *Irish Times* pointed out in 1916: 'No man feels exactly comfortable walking through the city with a big bag of clubs slung across his shoulder.'

(There was also another reason for this: in May, a number of sporting goods stores had been looted during the Dublin Insurrection with the theft of many hundreds of golf clubs and balls. *Golfing* magazine noted caustically that parks and sports fields were filled as 'the game enjoyed a sudden increase in popularity among certain youth of the city'.)

Few courses, however, were in a fit state to play on, in Dublin or anywhere else. With many clubs contributing to the war effort by turning over all or part of the course for the growing of vegetables or wheat, the condition of the remaining holes was understandably patchy. Upkeep now relied on the goodwill of retired members who were brought in to help with mowing the greens or raking the bunkers, but newspapers were carrying worrying headlines like 'Golf courses for the plough', and few clubs survived untouched.

Among the worst affected were the East Coast clubs: barbed wire and minefields replaced manicured tees and greens at Felixstowe, Aldeburgh and Yarmouth. In 1916, the club at Woking in Surrey faced an uncertain future – the Commanding Officer of the 1st London Division demanded the right to carry out manoeuvres on the tree-lined course, using horse-drawn artillery. Showing commendable cunning, the committee agreed to cooperate before making every officer an Honorary Member with an invitation to play the course any time they wished! Not surprisingly, the officers took up the offer, manoeuvres were cancelled, and the course survives to this day.

Walton Heath in Surrey was another golf club that had friends in high places. A fast running heath and heather course with wide fairways and perfect drainage, it was ideal ground for an artillery range but was deemed unsuitable for military use – a fortunate coincidence, since Munitions-Minister-turned-Prime Minister David Lloyd George and Winston Churchill were both regular visitors throughout the war! While the course was closed for the duration, the clubhouse remained open, as did the kitchens which were supplied with vegetables grown on a small plot of land near the pro's shop along with pork and bacon from their own small herd of pigs! Sadly, tragedy was to strike this elegant club: of 120 greens staff, caddies and other workers, only a handful would return from the war. The head green keeper, Mr McNiece, was among those killed in action.

Royal Wimbledon Golf Club, near the centre of London, was another that survived despite the privations of war. The 2nd, 15th and 16th holes were given over for food production, but the club could have lost many more holes had it not been for nearby Warren Farm. Having purchased the farm some

*A wounded officer from the Western Front follows the play at
Luton Hoo in 1916, with the aid of a pony carriage.*

years before in order to enlarge the golf course, they were able
to put it to good use growing vegetables and raising dairy
cattle. The farmhouse was utilised as a refuge for escaped
Belgian refugees, while the main clubhouse was made available during weekdays to convalescent non-commissioned
officers who were allowed to play bowls and putt.

The Royal Mid-Surrey course also struggled to stay open
throughout the war. Announcing that soldiers of any nation-
ality (except German and Austrian) would be welcome to
play free of charge, the Richmond club went out of its way to
provide care for wounded officers. From January 1916, they
offered tea and sandwiches every Friday afternoon to any
injured officer being treated at the nearby Red Cross Hospital.
In summer putting competitions were also arranged, which,
the acting club secretary reported to *Golf Monthly*, proved to
be a huge success: 'Wheel chairs are provided for those who
cannot walk and many heroes who have lost both their legs
have taken part with enthusiasm in such sporting contests.'

Account books for Royal Mid-Surrey in 1917 show a
substantial loss, especially on catering; but they also reveal

the sum of £379 paid out to the families of serving caddies and £167 to the families of serving green-keepers. This 'all pull together' mentality, typical of British golfers at the time, was commended as highly patriotic by *Golf Illustrated*. Soon after this, a Zeppelin raid over Burton-on-Trent in the English Midlands dropped two large bombs on the local golf course where naval officers were playing. Rather than terrifying the

THE AMENDED GOLF-COURSE.

local population – which it could so easily have done – the *Burton Mail* newspaper noted that the club had written to the R&A trying to clarify whether any ball landing in the craters should be considered 'rub of the green' or 'ground under repair'!

Further north, the Royal Lytham and St Annes course remained relatively unscathed – despite criticism by the author H. G. Wells that 'golf is taking up a great deal of land that would otherwise be available for grazing'. The nearby Dormy House provided accommodation not only for visiting members but also for convalescent officers, and the club grew its own produce in a vegetable patch next to Tom Simpson's professional's shop. This proved such a success that the innovative club secretary, T. Pym Williamson, wrote to the National Food Controller in 1917 asking whether 'potatoes grown on the premises could be served more than the one regulation day a week?' Turning his attention to the acute shortage of golf balls, he purchased 15 dozen at the club's expense so that visiting golfers would have something to play with. Justifying the exorbitant cost of £15. 17 shillings, he commented: 'What do you expect people to use – pebbles from the beach?'

The Royal Horse Guards set up a machine-gun position during infantry practice on Sandy Lodge golf course near London.

With much of the war being fought out in the trenches in faraway France and Belgium, Scotland fared better than it would two decades later in World War II. But from 1915 to 1917 a number of clubs fell foul of local authorities that seemed determined to grow crops on land previously used for golf. In December 1915, the Glasgow Sheriff Court rebuked Alexandra Golf Club for preferring to go to court rather than pay the trifling amount of £1 claimed by a farmer whose land adjoined the course for damage done to his crops by golfers looking for lost golf balls. In the words of Sheriff Lyel, 'Golf was after all only a sport, a pastime, a recreation, while agriculture was still the principal industry of the nation and golfers should bear in mind, should it ever come to be a question between the two, golf must go.'

A similar problem arose at Crail on the East Coast, where the Balcomie Links were acquired by the local council for the purpose of planting vegetables and only survived after the President of the Board of Agriculture announced in January 1917 that 'the cultivation of golf courses should be left to a later date'. A number of other courses were requisitioned by the Army as artillery ranges, such as the Portland course at Troon which was used for grenade practice.

*After the menfolk had left Britain for the Western Front, many
a woman filled the shortage of greenkeepers.*

St Andrews itself had a relatively 'good war' despite the
furious amount of military activity taking place in and around
the town. In September 1914, forced to cancel its popular
Autumn Meeting (a longstanding competition that had taken
place during the years of Waterloo and Crimea), the 'Home of
Golf' revealed a certain level of paranoia after a German spy
was caught making sketches on the Old Course! The unfortunate individual, who turned out to be a golfer-turned-
amateur-watercolourist, was subsequently arrested and
frogmarched back to the clubhouse over half a mile away,
accompanied by the burly figure of legendary golf professional
Andra' Kirkaldy. The suspect's ears must have been burning as
the former Scottish Highlander 'informed the suspect in his
best vernacular what he thought of the Kaiser, of all that is
German and what would happen to the Head of the
Fatherland if he met up with him on the links!'

Apart from being arrested for spying the biggest problem
facing golfers north of the border during World War I was
the increasingly poor state of the links. With many Scottish
green-keepers enlisting, quality staff were at a real premium;

Gullane in East Lothian agreed to pay a retaining half-wage to eight members of staff who had joined up in December 1914. (The committee later rescinded this decision in June 1915 because the war went on longer than expected.) As a temporary measure hundreds of sheep were purchased to keep the grass down at courses at Muirfield, Luffness and Dunbar. As the acting secretary at North Berwick reported in 1916, 'the possibility of the links reverting back to its wild and natural state had been contained'.

By Easter 1917, as the war dragged on into a third bloody year, most British golf courses were in daily use; and with so many green-keeping staff away, local women were employed to help with maintenance. By the end of the war, male golfers had become so accustomed to seeing women about the course that many of the barriers that existed prior to 1914 were effectively broken down. Although there would be no visible increase in the number of women who actually played golf after the war, those who did found their conditions much improved, areas of the clubhouse now being given over to them along with extra playing privileges.

Legendary *Times* golf correspondent and noted author Bernard Darwin was a lieutenant in the Army Ordinance Department during World War I.

HOW TO PLAY IN A GAS MASK:

Put on the gas mask and continue to play as before. Endeavour to refrain from conversation (*Next month* – How to play golf in a Tin Hat.).

Golf Monthly, September 1939

CHAPTER VI

The Niblick Brigade

Such was the lightning speed of the German advance in 1914 that many British subjects working on the Continent, including a number of golf professionals, were forced into making daring escapes. Barely one step ahead of the Kaiser's army was Albert Tingey. A founding member of the PGA, he established the first golf school in Paris in 1913 before moving to nearby Fontainebleau twelve months later. Arriving in Dieppe just ahead of the Germans, he felt strongly that British golf should do all they could to fight tyranny and in August 1914 conceived the idea of the 'Niblick Brigade'.

Inspired by Lord Kitchener's 'Your country needs you!' call-to-arms, Tingey and fellow Professional Golfers Association member Charles Mayo believed that golf professionals and their assistants should be able to join the Army together and fight side by side in France. (The British Government encouraged men from the same city, town or even village to enlist as a group, which became a major factor in the death of many rural communities as entire regiments were wiped out in the conflict.) The idea was given full support by the PGA and backed by fellow members George Duncan, William Robertson Reith and Wilfred Reid, the only qualification being that each man should be a bachelor and have no dependants. Twenty-six bachelor professionals responded to the call, along with many married men who were turned away. It was suggested that professionals too old for active service should join the voluntary police force while

*The golf professionals and assistants who volunteered
to form the Niblick Brigade gather at Nelson's Column in
London's Trafalgar Square.*

those passed fit to serve were drafted into the King's Royal
Rifles at Winchester Barracks.

In an emotional gathering on 12 September 1914, the
golfers met for lunch at Gatti's Restaurant in London immediately before adjourning to the recruiting office. Assembling
for a group photograph among the pigeons of Trafalgar
Square, they were joined by representatives of the golf industry including Mr Mathieson, editor of *Golf Monthly*. Having
accepted the 'King's shilling' paid out to all new recruits, many
of them headed off to the post office at Charing Cross where
the wires were kept busy sending farewell messages.

Thus the 'Niblick Brigade' was born; and, realising what a
wonderful opportunity it was to raise the profile of the humble golf professional, Private Albert S. Tingey of Number 2
Company, Royal Rifle Brigade began writing a regular update
on their activities for *Golf Monthly*. Offering mundane details
about what food they ate, how many miles they marched
that week and what time they got up in the morning, these
patriotically flavoured reports lasted well into 1915.

Eager to keep up morale, *Golfing* magazine began its coverage of the 1916 season by publishing the 'Golfer's Alphabet' written by a serving officer in the Niblick Brigade 'somewhere' in Flanders:

A is for the Army of golfers and pros,
Who in Greece and in Flanders are facing our foes.
B is the Bombs that we're using for balls,
Our opponents 'lie dead' wheresoever one falls.
C is our Corps —not a rubber-core [golf ball] now,
But the pride of the Army as French will allow.
D is the Driver —who comes with his car,
To keep up our stock of munitions of war.
E is the Expert, our line who determines,
He lays out the course and we lay out the Germans.
F is the Flagstick that through thick and thin,
We'll carry and plant on the walls of Berlin.
G is the Game that we know how to play,
However our opponents may wander astray.
H is the Hazards, from snipers and shell,
But as long as we're careful we do pretty well.
I is the Iron that entered our soul,
When a shot through our frying pan drilled a neat hole.
J is a Joke that is capital fun,
When we aim at the sniper and 'hole out in one'.
K is the Kultur that's held by the ghouls [Germans]
As a perfect excuse to keep breaking the rules.
L is the language we use in the trenches,
Through long practice at golf we astonish the Frenchies.
M is the Mashie-approaches we play,
For the Huns are not more than a chip away.
N is the Niblick we carry about,
To dig ourselves in —and dig our boots out [of the mud].
O is the Odd we at first had to play,
But the Huns playing 'three more' the rest of the way.
P is the Pitch that we chose for our tent,
It is weak as to headroom but cheap as to rent.
Q is the Quarry that shelters our band,
And we're all full of grit for there's plenty of sand.
R is the Run-up when we're told to advance,
And the rage of the foe through whose trenches we prance.

S is the stymie we laid for the Hun,
Who 'putted' [marched] for Calais but found himself done.
T is the Trench that we carried one day,
Out driving the Germans who stood in our way.
U is the U-boat we dodged coming over,
For we 'putted' first and was 'run-down' off Dover.
V is the Victory we're going to score,
We feel we can do it by five-up and four.
W the Winners, who someday you'll see,
With their clubs once, again upon No. 1 tee.
X is the Extra delight we shall know,
When once more to the links we are able to go.
Y is for Ypres – we're stationed near there,
And the town's best described as 'ground under repair'.
Z is for Zeps [Zeppelin airships]. If they fly over the town,
We give them a lofted shot – that brings them down

Back on the front line, news was becoming increasingly grim. With the list of war casualties growing day by day, *Golf Monthly* quietly dropped Albert Tingey's detailed updates in favour of regular one-paragraph news items penned by Lance Corporal William Eastland, who described how in January 1916 'the Niblick Brigade are still going strong despite trenches waist-deep in water and dug-outs collapsing in the floods'. Then in March came the news that the Niblick Brigade had suffered its first casualty:

> *Rifleman Herbert Line, formerly assistant at Le Touquet, has been struck in the face by a bullet which ricocheted off the ammunition pouch of another recruit. Another rifleman who went to Line's assistance was hit through the lung and died before reaching hospital but Line himself was able, with the help of stretcher bearers, to walk to the dressing station. We are happy to say that he is already on the fairway to recovery.*

Shying away from bad news, *Golfing* magazine reported in May 1916 that a 'golf course' had been designed and built 'in

*The Niblick Brigade, now officially complete, pose for a group
photograph in front of London's National Portrait Gallery.*

the Ypres salient by our own sub-editor Ramsey Ross'. Then in
August, *The Daily Chronicle* reported another one which had
been 'laid out behind the firing line in Flanders by former
Scottish International, Tom Fernie'. As if that were not
impressive enough, a 9-hole course was designed and built
near Army Headquarters 'somewhere in France' by a former
sport journalist attached to the General Staff, Rifleman A. T.
Gardiner. The conditions would 'shock the soul of a real
golfer', he wrote. He sent his description of the course to a
number of British newspapers who lapped up the story as
evidence of how well the war was going.

    With razor wire used to define each fairway and bomb
craters filled with rainwater doubling-up as water hazards,
Gardiner described the course as 'fearful'. Appealing to the
British public for golf balls because they were 'deuced expen-
sive for a Tommy's limited means', he thought playing golf
within sound of the enemy guns would raise morale and 'vary
the monotony of active warfare and help keep himself and

others fit for action'. Applauding this 'ambitious attempt to introduce the Royal and Ancient Game so near the actual fighting line', the *Daily Chronicle* reported that 'work at headquarters is strenuous and continuous, so that outdoor recreation of some sort becomes a necessity for both officers and men'.

In May 1916 the future prime minister J. Ramsay MacDonald was expelled from Moray Golf Club on the grounds that his sentiments were pro-German and his attitude defeatist. *Golfing* magazine joined in the attack on him, saying, 'All honour to those who turned him out! Golf is a great game and those who play it are sportsmen and Ramsay *und* MacDonald knows nothing of sportsmanship.'

Attempting to keep up the patriotic line that 'all was well on the Western Front', the soon-to-be-defunct *Golf Illustrated* published a number of letters revealing that golf was a regular topic of conversation in the trenches and not just among the Niblick Brigade. The first, from Sergeant Harry Fulford in September 1916, recounted that

> *Whenever one of us has been home, the boys we see on our return wish to hear of nothing so much as the courses played upon, whom we met, whom we beat, and were beaten by. And the most ordinary story of the most ordinary match, such as the bores used to tell about continually in peacetime, is listened to with as much wonder as it were a story of the Arabian Nights and we were children again.*

The patriotic line that the noble 'Tommy' had nothing more to concern himself with than golf matches back home was taken up by *Golfing*, who published a letter from Charles Willmott, former club pro at Woburn Sands, a few weeks later:

> *Sir —I received my copy of GOLFING all safe. One doesn't get much time out here to think about what is going on at home but it does one good to see GOLFING and know the*

old game is still in existence. It would take a good deal of
strafing to kill it don't you think?

> Yours Faithfully,
> 73044 Cpl. Chas. Willmott
> 14th Army Corps
> Headquarters Signal Company
> B.E.F. Belgium.

In August 1916 his fellow professionals were caught up in a
so-called 'Big Push' against the German lines. Reporting that the
Niblick Brigade had survived heavy shelling throughout the
summer months without loss, Eastland described how 'the battalion advanced most gallantly over land ploughed by the
artillery and swept by the enemy's machine guns amidst a hail of
bullets'. Although none of the 'Niblicks' were killed at this time,
the list of wounded from this one offensive reveals a catalogue
of injuries that would ruin many a fine professional career:

Sgt. James Scarth (Doncaster Golf Club) wounded in legs;
Sgt. Fred Jolly (Beckenham Golf Club) wounded in arm;
Acting-Corporal Seward (Beckenham Golf Club) wounded
  in leg;
Acting-Corporal C. Macey (Littlehampton Golf Club)
  wounded in shoulder;
Rifleman Robertson (Leicestershire Golf Club) wounded in
  mouth;
Rifleman Towlson (Thorpe Hall Golf Club) wounded in
  hand.

And death itself was just around the corner. Like many
fighting units the Niblick Brigade became increasingly depleted,
and of those listed above only Scarth and Macey survived the
war to take up professional's jobs at Bolton and Rother respectively. From the start of 1917 caddies, green keepers and former club makers were added to the Brigade, but the death toll

A gently therapeutic game of golf for shell-shocked casualties of World War I was a common activity at convalescent hospitals like this one at Hatfield.

kept mounting, with Rifleman Eastland also falling victim to enemy fire.

There was little sympathy for anyone who exhibited an unwillingness to die for King and Country, and hundreds of British soldiers were executed for desertion or cowardice in the face of the enemy. In June 1917 the poet Siegfried Sassoon was

banished to a sanatorium in Scotland after refusing to rejoin his
regiment, the Welsh Fusiliers, back in France. A winner of the
Military Cross, he had been invalided back to England after
receiving a bullet wound in the leg. His opposition to the war,
an offence punishable by firing squad, was both vocal and heart-
felt: he had lost his brother, best friend and two cousins to the
conflict in the previous few weeks. Criticising the Government
for not doing enough to end the war, he welcomed the prospect
of the public debate that a court martial would bring; but this
was thwarted by a Military Medical Board who effectively
declared him insane. He was packed off to Craiglockhart
Hospital for the shell-shocked, near Edinburgh – and it was
there that he rediscovered his love of golf.

Having thrown his medal into the mouth of the River
Mersey while walking alongside the golf course at Formby
near Blackpool, he recalled one of his many pleasurable
rounds at nearby Mortonhall in his book, *The Complete
Memoirs of George Sherston*:

> *When played seriously, even golf can, I suppose, claim to
> be 'an epitome of human life…' I wasn't worrying much
> about the War when I'd hit a perfect tee-shot up the
> charming vista which was the fairway to the first green..
> How easy it felt! I scarcely seemed to be gripping the club
> at all. Afternoon sunshine was slanting through the golden
> brown beeches and at last I knew what it was like to hit
> the ball properly. 'I suppose I'm getting too keen on the
> game,' I thought as I bicycled home to the Hydro at the end
> of some such afternoon, when I'd been sampling one of
> the delightfully unfrequented links which the war had
> converted into Arcadian solitudes.*

Sadly the recuperative benefits of empty wartime golf
courses were only available to a select few, but the game continued to provide many volunteers right up to the end. With
the Niblick Brigade leading the way, Hull Golf Club in the

northeast of England provided enough men to form the Hull Volunteer Battalion, while in November 1916 70 members of Sidcup Golf Club in Kent likewise joined up en masse. Another such unit was the so-called 'Sportsman Brigade', made up of amateur golfers and cricket players. Its most famous combatant, the irrepressible Lance Corporal Ernest Jones, was to become one of the best-known golf coaches in America in the post-war era. Wounded by a grenade that led to his right leg being amputated in February 1916, he proved a reluctant patient and was challenging the surgeons to a game of golf within weeks of his operation. By August, the British-born golfer had even penned an article for *Golfing* showing how to play golf on one leg!

Of course, not every professional was away fighting in the war. Those considered too old or infirm to enlist continued to give lessons and repair clubs at golf clubs up and down the country while the 'Great Triumvirate' of Harry Vardon, James Braid and John Henry Taylor did their 'bit' as best they could. It was noted in 1915 that Vardon spent his time milking cows on a farm near his home in Totteridge, Hertfordshire while Taylor worked in a Red Cross canteen in Richmond, Surrey. Thirty miles further south James Braid worked in an armaments factory near his home club of Walton Heath in Surrey. In between these unglamorous duties they would take part in an exhausting series of exhibition matches, raising thousands

1912 British Open Champion and 1920 United States Open Champion, Edward Ray played in countless wartime exhibition matches with Vardon, Braid and Taylor before attempting to enlist in January 1916. A lifelong pipe smoker, he was rejected on medical grounds despite being 2 years under military age. In between exhibition matches he worked in a munitions factory, like Vardon.

British Open winner in 1907, Arnaud Massy, was wounded in the thigh by an exploding shell at Verdun in 1916 and taken to a battlefield hospital where he made a full recovery.

of pounds for the Red Cross and other war charities. With petrol in short supply they would travel by train to the various venues, where they would play an 18-hole foursomes match in the morning and the same again in the afternoon before auctioning off various prizes donated by the members. Joined on the road by a selection of former Open champions including Jack White (discharged from the London Scottish Regiment in March 1916 owing to ill heath) and Edward Ray (rejected on medical grounds in 1915), they continued these hugely popular matches right up to the end of the war.

Among the many professionals from the Commonwealth who contributed to the final victory over Germany were the New Zealand PGA – 6 members out of 13 signing up in 1916 to fight in Turkey. Along with those from the paid ranks, many thousands of amateur golfers from Canada, India and Australia hastened to the enlisting centres. Vancouver Golf Club had 40 members who enlisted, while Royal Montreal and Royal Ottawa boasted 70 active members each. In Australia 24 members of Brisbane Golf Club went to fight in the Dardanelles in February 1915 with barely a handful returning;

in December 1916 a poem was read out by the club captain in commemoration of their huge sacrifice. The extract quoted here could apply to any golfer who ever went to war:

> They're fighting for us and fighting well, in air, on land
>   and sea,
> And they drive through a hell of bursting shell, from a
>   trench as their starting tee.
> The niblicks they ween are bayonets keen and well they
>   wield the same,
> And we honour each lad in khaki clad, for the way he's
>   played the game.
>
> Our cause is right tho' war is wrong or so it seems to me,
> Who am I but a simple singer of song of modest low
>   degree.
> But whether it's war or whether it's golf, we honour each
>   man's name,
> According to how he acts right now and the way he plays
>   his game.

Raising funds for the Red Cross, Alexander Carstairs of St Andrews donated an ancient gutta-percha golf ball for a charity auction at Sunningdale in November 1916. Described as a 'dirty brown and rather disreputable object', it dated from 1848 and was among the first gutta balls ever used. It was bought by Mr Gordon Campbell, Chairman of the Meat and Allied Appeal Committee, who auctioned it off three weeks later at Smithfield Meat Market in London. Standing on a butcher's block, he explained what an important part the gutta had played in the development of the game and, according to one reporter, 'touched the hearts and minds of those present with his eloquence'. The item fetched a massive £108 (the equivalent of £35,000 today), the highest price ever paid for a single golf ball.

CHAPTER VII

Prisoners of War
Ruhleben Country Club

AT THE OUTBREAK of World War I there were a large number of British golf professionals working overseas in France, Belgium, Holland and even Germany. While many managed to scramble back to England, some did not, including a remarkable character named Cuthbert Butchart. A noted teaching professional in Berlin since 1911, the Carnoustie-born pro was designated a 'non German National' and banished to a newly built prisoner-of-war camp at Ruhleben in November 1914. (About 5000 British subjects were living in Germany at the outbreak of war. All were questioned and told that as long as they reported weekly to the local police they would remain free. But when the German authorities learned that some 30,000 of their fellow citizens had been rounded up and interned in Britain they decided to follow suit.)

The regime at Ruhleben, a former racecourse in the Berlin suburb of Spandau, was fairly relaxed compared with the notorious prisoner-of-war camps of World War II. With the stables providing accommodation for 365 men, the inmates were effectively left to govern themselves with a token force of aged German soldiers to guard them. And while the Dutch established a library, the 21-strong contingent of British professionals immediately set about making life more tolerable by building a 5-hole golf course!

The course was laid out on waste ground within the racing circuit, and Butchart was appointed Honorary Secretary

*The members of the 'Ruhleben Country Club' pictured in their World
War I internment camp near Berlin. C.S. Butchart, the club's founder,
Honorary Secretary and Treasurer, is seated far left.*

and Treasurer of the newly-named 'Ruhleben Country Club'.
He established a morale-boosting schedule of tournaments,
with the results published in the prisoners' own magazine!
Providing regular lessons to anyone wishing to take up the
game, he appealed to the British public to send clubs and balls
via the Red Cross. In a letter to *Golfing* magazine in June 1916,
he described how popular golf had become and explained
how tee-times had to be strictly regulated among the 73 members as the course was 'quite busy between the hours of 8.00
and 9.00 in the morning'.

Released in 1919, Butchart remained in Berlin for another
two years, before taking up a teaching post at Biltmore
Country Club in New York. He died in 1955 aged 79.

1920 British Open champion George Duncan played many Red Cross
Exhibition matches before and after joining the Royal Flying
Corps in 1916.

CHAPTER VIII

America ponders whether to golf or not . . .

O N 6 APRIL 1917, the United States of America entered
World War I.

With an Expeditionary Force under the command of
General Pershing setting sail for Europe on 28 June, the call-
to-arms by President Wilson was taken up enthusiastically by
the American people who, emboldened by patriotic senti-
ment, determined their 'boys' would lack for absolutely nothing. Fund-raising events were organised all over the country,
with the nation's golfers playing a leading role. So-called
'Liberty Tournaments' were organised with 485 golf clubs in
44 states grossing a total of $72,000 in war bond subscriptions
on one weekend alone. Substituting Liberty Bonds and War
Savings Stamps for more traditional tournament prizes, members would then donate half of their monthly medal entry fee
towards a fund for buying army ambulances. It seemed this
was a war America was determined to win.

Another aspect of this frantic fund-raising activity was the
lessening of the guilt that many golfers felt about playing their
favourite sport in time of war. Woodrow Wilson, a golfer
himself, had encouraged his countrymen to continue playing
sport because it made a 'real contribution to the national
defence' by keeping its citizens physically fit and alert. Yet
there was still a faintly unpatriotic feel to playing golf when so
many people were fighting and dying in far-off France and
Belgium. Like many British clubs, a number of private golf

President Woodrow Wilson: not easily put off a game of golf by the outbreak of World War I.

clubs – especially in the New York and Boston areas – gave up part of their course for the growing of wheat and vegetables.

Probably no one really thought that American lives would be saved by sacrificing a few holes, but at least it helped when faced with the question whether 'to golf or not to golf?', which was proving a real dilemma. Even the President had to ask close adviser Colonel Edward M. House whether playing golf would make a bad impression. 'I don't think the American people feel that the President should do anything trivial at a time like this,' House answered, before they both headed off for a secret game of pool in the White House basement. But Wilson was not so easily put off and was back on the links soon afterwards – although a game of golf was no simple undertaking when accompanied, as he was, not just by a caddie but by two motorcycle policemen and nine Secret Service men.

Raising money for a number of war charities, President Wilson regularly attended exhibition matches in and around the Washington DC area. Accompanied by stars of the game such as Walter Hagen, Jim Barnes and Chick Evans, he would autograph balls for the post-match charity auction which often sold for as much as $500. He knew how much his presence boosted morale; but a fund-raising event at the White House almost threatened his budding golf career. Persuaded to take a ride in a battle-scarred British tank named *Britannia* in April 1918, he mistakenly grabbed a red-hot exhaust pipe that severely burned his right hand. With his right arm in

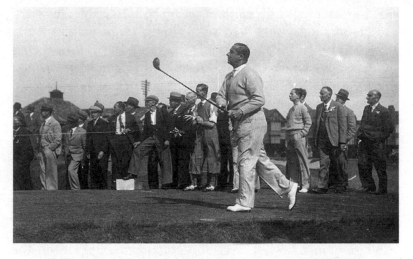

*Walter Hagen, who clocked up 75,000 miles playing charity
golf matches across the US during World War I.*

a sling for several weeks, he began by hitting golf balls with
his left on the White House lawn and became surprisingly
efficient, prompting his wife Edith to comment: 'Woodrow is
becoming the greatest one-arm champion in the world.'

A number of changes had to be made in the President's
routine because of security. Shadowed by the Secret Service
wherever he played, he demanded they know something
about golf etiquette before even stepping out on the course.
Even then he ordered them to stand out of sight behind trees
and bushes at a discreet distance while he was hitting the ball.

Wilson declined to play through other golfers despite
numerous invitations (especially from other politicians looking to curry favour with the boss), and indeed steadfastly
refused to accept favours of any kind, especially when it came
to golf. On one famous occasion Dr Garfield, head of the
Government's Commission on Fuel, contacted the White
House with an offer he thought would delight the President.
Instrumental in banning the use of fuel at golf and country
clubs in the autumn of 1918, he 'wished the President to know

that he would take pleasure in seeing to it that the necessary exemptions are granted to the country clubs at which the President played golf'. Rejecting the offer, Wilson instructed his private secretary Joseph P. Tumulty to reply, 'that I would not for anything have him [Dr Garfield] make any exception with regard to the country clubs at which I play'.

Following the example of the R&A, who cancelled both the British Open and the Amateur Championships in 1915, the United States Golf Association 'postponed' their own Open and Amateur events on 23 April 1917. The recently formed Professional Golfers Association then followed suit by halting the PGA Championship after consulting with its biggest star, Walter Hagen. But top names were encouraged to compete in exhibition matches all over the country to help raise the game's profile, and demand for their services was unprecedented. As championship golf became a thing of the past, the USGA responded to public demand by staging 'The Open Patriotic Tournament' in June 1917. (The reason for this rather clumsy title was that tennis had already scheduled a 'Patriotic Open Tournament' a few weeks earlier in New York.)

Replacing the cancelled US Open, the event was played at Whitemarsh Valley Country Club, Chestnut Hill, Pennsylvania. All gate receipts went to the Red Cross and, as he had come up with the original idea, it was only fair that exiled Scot Jock Hutchison took the top prize on a score of 292, beating Tom McNamara into second by 7 shots. The tournament proved a big hit with everyone and inspired a host of wartime challenge matches between the great stars of the day, similar to those played in the United Kingdom between Vardon, Braid and Taylor.

By far the biggest draw was Walter Hagen. Travelling all over the country in the cause of charity, he is known to have clocked up over 75,000 miles in *Madam X* – his sixteen-cylinder Cadillac. Exempted from military duty because of his marriage in 1917, he would often arrive in town after a night at the wheel before pegging it up on the first tee not knowing – or indeed caring —who he was up against. And whether it was battle-hardened veterans like Jim Barnes and Johnny McDermott or amateur-turned-professionals like Jesse Guilford and Mike Brady, the flamboyant star rarely lost. After all, the crowd had come to see 'Sir' Walter and he considered it 'unpatriotic' to finish second best.

Not that America's top amateur golfers were ignored. Held in far greater esteem than many of their professional colleagues —with the possible exception of Hagen —three of the past four winners of the US Open had come from the unpaid ranks: Francis Ouimet (1913), Jerome Travers (1915) and Charles 'Chick' Evans (1916). From mid-1917 onwards, they simply barnstormed around the country, playing exhibition matches – often against professional opponents – and soliciting for donations on behalf of the Red Cross and other war charities. Their schedule must have been gruelling: arriving by train or bus the night before, they would play a 36-hole match, hang around for the charity auction afterwards, then take the late-night sleeper on to the next venue.

The ball is near the right toe, note the tense grip.   His body is poised for the application of all his strength.   The finish is like that for a full drive.

Wartime golf barnstormer Jerome Travers demonstrates the art of the backswing.

His feet are close and his body bends far over.   A flat upswing between elbow and shoulder.   The follow through is far for this class of shot.

Francis Ouimet, controversially stripped of his amateur status
until he joined the US Army in 1918.

Another hugely popular draw in golf-hungry America was the so-called 'Dixie Kids'. This outfit featured a 15-year-old prodigy named Bobby Jones, who was joined on the road by three other young stars: Perry Adair, Elaine Rosenthal and Alexa Stirling. Dressed in red Swiss Guard berets, they would crisscross the country competing against each other, or local champions, in a range of fourball and Scotch foursome matches on behalf of the Red Cross.

A boyhood rival of Jones from Atlanta, Adair was considered one of the most talented juniors in America, while Alexa had already won the Women's National Championship aged just 19. Considered the best woman golfer in the Midwest, Elaine Rosenthal would partner Bobby one day and Perry the next, before joining Alexa in a 'battle of the sexes' event which also proved popular. Occasionally, the girls would sit things out and watch the 'Dixie Boys' battle it out with golfers twice their age before heading off to the next stop on their whistle-stop tour of the country.

In June 1918, Bobby Jones was invited to take part in a

series of exhibition matches with reigning US Open and Amateur champion Charles Evans, after Evans's regular playing partner, Warren Wood, fell ill. At such events it was commonplace for members to pay hundreds of dollars for the privilege of caddying for Chick Evans or some other golfing star like Hagen, Travers or Hutchison. Clubs and balls used by these players would then be sold off for charity, with a record $35,000 raised by the members of Lake Shore Country Club in Chicago in 1918.

Probably the best golfer in the world at the time, Evans raised over $300,000 for charity, having declared at the outset of war that he 'would enter no tournaments and play no public golf except for the Red Cross'. Yet it must have undermined his confidence to watch how easily the talented youngster handled such high-profile matches. Realising he would have to face Jones head-to-head one day could not have been a comfortable experience. (They would finally meet in the final of US Amateur at Minikahda in 1927, where Jones effectively ended his career, winning by 8&7.)

The Western Golf Association, which had organised many exhibition matches for the Red Cross, had also attracted a huge amount of criticism – not least from the United States Golf Association – for maintaining a full schedule of tournaments. Finally the WGA bowed to the inevitable and cancelled its controversial list of events for 1917. Peace between the two organisations was finally achieved. As *The New York Times* commented in February, 'since it was the consensus of the country that golf fixtures should be discontinued until the war is over, the Western body felt itself duty bound to the edict of the nation'.

It was not the first time the WGA and USGA had locked horns: in October 1916, the USGA stripped Francis Ouimet of his amateur status after he announced his attention to open a sporting goods store with his buddy, Jack Sullivan. Ouimet had been ranked by a committee of magazine editors as the second best amateur in the country behind Jerome Travers (the remaining positions in the top 10 were filled by Robert

Charles H. Ward, two-times Vardon Trophy winner.

Gardner in 3rd place, Charles Evans in 4th, Maxwell Marston in 5th, Walter Travis in 6th, John Anderson in 7th, D. E. Sawyer in 8th, H. Chandler Egan in 9th and William Fownes in 10th).

With the USGA defining a 'professional' as anyone who engaged in business that traded on his or her reputation as a golfer, the shy Bostonian was banned from competing in any officially sanctioned amateur championship with immediate effect. That was where the problems really began. Embodying the very ideal of the American amateur, not only had Ouimet defeated the 'unbeatable' Harry Vardon and Edward Ray in a play-off to win the 1913 US Open at Brookline, he had also turned down a fortune in commercial endorsements precisely because he specifically wanted to remain an amateur. Equally, as a man of honour, he had given his word to Sullivan that he would partner him and no pressure from the USGA would persuade him to break it. Not surprisingly, the USGA's decision brought a hail of criticism – not least from the Western Golf Association, who threatened to break away completely.

Walter Travis, a three-time Amateur Champion and the 'Old Man' of American golf, had also fallen foul of the new guidelines because of his golf-course designing activities. Rarely losing an opportunity to criticise USGA President Woodward and his committee, he lambasted them for their 'intense conservatism' and for being totally unrepresentative of America's golfers. Backed by sport journalist W. O. McGeehan, he summed up the feelings of many when he wrote, 'the men who compose the USGA seemed to believe that there was some intensified stigma attached to the word *professional...*'

Feeling that a great injustice had been inflicted upon him, Ouimet reluctantly obeyed the order not to compete in any amateur event, hoping against hope that the USGA would eventually change its mind. After six long months his patience finally snapped in July 1917, when he entered and won the Western Amateur. His accepting this invitation from the WGA to compete in their premier event meant the battle lines had been well and truly drawn between the two organisations, and

*Cadets at West Point military academy were encouraged to take
advantage of its golf links laid out among the rolling country
the Hudson River.*

it would be some time before reconciliation could be achieved.
As for Ouimet, he continued to play golf before being accepted into the Army and billeted at Camp Devens, near Boston.
Not long afterwards, in October 1917, he was reinstated as an
amateur by the new USGA president, Howard W. Perrin.
Justifying his decision, Perrin said there was no longer any
conflict of interest, as all connections with the sporting goods
firm had been severed once Ouimet had entered the armed
forces.

By the time World War I came to a welcome close in
November 1918, the image of golf had undergone a complete
transformation —especially the professional game. While still
relatively young, golf in the United States had enhanced its
patriotic credentials and would be forever associated with the
highest of sporting ideals. Receiving more newspaper coverage than ever, both *The American Golfer* magazine and *Golf
Illustrated* were flourishing with regular updates about the
British game. Typical of these reports was an inspirational

poem published in *The American Golfer* in February 1918 entitled 'To the Kaiser!'

> *We were out of sorts and practice when you challenged us*
> *to play,*
> *Because you won the first two holes you thought you won*
> *the Day.*
> *But soon we found our game and now how do you like the*
> *score?*
> *For we're on our drive and mettle and we're also on our*
> *form.*
> *Don't put your trust in bunkers and submarines – don't*
> *think*
> *To stymie us: the former we shall fill, the latter we shall*
> *sink.*
> *Your bogey don't alarm us, nor the dirty little way*
> *Of your caddie 'Little Willie' who to steal the ball essays.*
> *The honor's lost: you've lost the match, for in 1918,*
> *We'll lay our second and your Highness dead upon the*
> *green.*
> *Your iron play may be excellent, you may be driving well,*
> *The fact is we'll be down in three while you'll be down in*
> *hell!*

The thousands of miles travelled by players like Walter
Hagen in the cause of charity helped give the humble professional golfer far higher status than in the pre-war period.
While raising a small fortune for the Red Cross, he and other
pro's had also managed to raise their social profile in an
increasingly status-conscious America; and in the decades that
followed, their situation would improve still further.

On the afternoon before the Armistice was declared, amateur legend Walter Travis was out playing an exhibition match
against his old rival, Findlay Douglas. Winning through in a
tight match, Travis generously auctioned off the legendary
aluminium-headed Schenectady putter he had used to

become the first American resident to win the British Amateur Championship back in 1904. Realising an incredible $1,700, this battered old club represented the passing of an era. Travis knew his day was over, while others like Evans and Ouimet could only reflect on those years lost to the war playing essentially meaningless exhibition matches.

For the average American golfer, life had changed little during those years. There had been shortages early in the war and a number of courses had been lost for good after being turned over for food production, but they were few and far between. In 1918, a survey showed that US golfers spent over $10 million on golf balls in that year alone – proof, if any proof were needed, that the 'war to end all wars' that had raged since 1914 had had little impact on daily life for the average American.

Golf itself, on the other hand, had a massive effect on the American economy, as a revealing 1916 commentary entitled *The Magnitude of Golf*, by George Fitch, showed:

> *America is a mighty country and any little thing in it, when multiplied into a national total, becomes an awe-inspiring total. Twenty years ago a few American enthusiasts were bombarding cows in a pasture while rows of solid citizens surrounded the fence and tapped their heads sadly as they watched them. Today half a million tired businessmen march out onto the 3000 golf courses of this country. If these men were to drive off together from a tee five miles long, they would mow down an approaching army of 50,000 men at one stroke!*
>
> *If they were to use their niblicks in the same place they would dig a canal 100 feet wide, ten feet deep and two miles long... If they were to drive off in turn, the last man would have to wait 176 years four months and three days for his number... Half a million dollars worth of golf balls are lost each Saturday against $345 worth that are found... The golf courses of America would cover 298,345 acres with a pond seven miles round... Golf has added a total of 543,768*

*years to the lives of its players but the exertion of getting
away from the office early on Saturdays has removed a total
of 552,876 years, thus leaving a loss of 8,892 years. It cost
about $25 to learn the game from a professional with those
wishing to join a good club from $50 to $200. Players
wishing to give up the game may have an arm and a leg
removed by any surgeon at reasonable rates...*

The war won, US soldiers returned home with horror
stories about gas attacks, death-filled trenches and whizz-bang
bombs; but it was quickly forgotten. This was a distant war
where the closest the average American came to the conflict
was reading sanitised reports from the front in his daily newspaper or golf magazine.

Sadly for them, the same could not be said about the
conflict to come.

The Professional Golfers' Association of America was formed in January
1916. In October, Cornishman Jim Barnes beat Scot Jock Hutchison to win
the inaugural PGA Championship at Siwanoy, taking the $500 first prize.

Tommy Armour was a legend in his own lifetime. Winner of the US Open,
US PGA and British Open, he became a renowned teacher and bestselling
author. Injured by an artillery shell during World War I, the 'Silver Scot' is
supposed to have leaped out of his tank before killing a German officer with
his bare hands. In 1922 he headed for America where, as the result of his war
injury, he played most of his professional career blind in one eye.

CHAPTER IX:

Golf between the Wars
1919 to 1938

HAILED AS 'the Prime Minister who beat the Germans', David Lloyd George enjoyed a period of enormous popularity at the end of World War I. Winning a crushing landslide election victory at the end of 1918, he returned to Downing Street on a wave of patriotic fervour, to take on the task of leading Britain into a new 'golden era'. Yet those who returned from the trenches of northern France expecting a better way of life found little had changed. The promised reforms in education, housing, health and transport remained unfulfilled, and through the 1920s and into the 1930s unemployment in the major industrial cities rose alarmingly and there was increasing social unrest as the gulf between rich and poor continued to widen.

The position of British golf reflected the wider situation. After struggling throughout the war years, the vast majority of courses were in poor condition and many private clubs hovered near bankruptcy as memberships dropped along with revenue. Championship golf should have returned in October 1919 with the Women's Amateur at Burnham and Berrow, but this was cancelled because of a national rail strike. Accordingly, all major events including the British Open — now the sole responsibility of the R&A —were delayed until the following year. Even the PGA was under threat until Edward Ray persuaded the Earl of Wilton to make a much-needed donation of £500. With secretary F. H. Brown killed on

active duty in 1915, the Association's affairs had gone into limbo until the appointment of lawyer Roland Perrins in 1919.

A letter to *Golf Illustrated* from five-time British Open winner John Henry Taylor predicted in 1917 that golf would play little importance in the rebuilding of British life after the war:

> *One certain effect of this war will be to reduce the*
> *interest and importance of professional golf tournaments.*
> *Perhaps this is all to the good. There is a feeling that far*
> *too much attention was given to it before and that it was*
> *not good for the game. I ought to add that I have heard no*
> *professional complain though they have been severely hit.*
> *They are a good-hearted and patriotic set of men...*

Painting a bleak picture, Taylor said how surprised he would be if the British Open Championship was held within three or four years of the war coming to a close. In the event it would be just two, as Cinque Ports in Deal was selected by the R&A to host the 55th playing of golf's oldest major in 1920. Nor had the Professional Golfers Association had been slow in arranging a 'major' tournament of their own: in 1919, a so-called 'Victory' Tournament was played at King's Park, Stirling. A 36-hole professionals-only event, it was intended to identify the stars of the future while putting a shot across the bows of the autocratic R&A who, in the PGA's opinion, had been dragging their collective feet about staging the British Open. In the United States competitive golf had already got under way, after a break of two years, with the US Open, PGA and US Amateur all scheduled for 1919. Why, the PGA wanted to know, was the Open lagging behind? Most of the great Scottish courses, including St Andrews, were in relatively good order, but no matter how much pressure was put on the R&A to set a date, answer came there none.

As the 1919 golf season got under way, the only question now was who would take up the mantle of the 'Great

Triumvirate'. Having dominated the game for over two decades before the war, Harry Vardon, 49, James Braid, 49, and J. H. Taylor, 48, were now considered past their best and not expected to win again. The same applied to Open-winning contemporaries like Sandy Herd, 51, Harold Hilton, 50, and even 42-year-old Ted Ray. So as a new era in golf approached, what British player would take their place? Would it be brilliant amateur-turned professional, Abe Mitchell? Or former Belgian and French Open champion George Duncan? Who would have the honour of winning the first important tournament after the war? The answer, when it came, surprised everyone.

Laurie B. Ayton was a little-known but hugely talented professional from St Andrews whose career had been severely disrupted by the war years. He had entered the British Open at Muirfield in 1912 against doctor's orders and, despite illness, had finished fifth. The following year he headed the qualifiers at Royal Liverpool before fading away in the later rounds. In 1914, he set a new course record of 64 at Brancaster in Norfolk which Bernard Darwin, writing in *The Times*, described as 'perfectly staggering'. The type of player who was always likely to shoot low scores if the mood caught him, Ayton had enlisted in the Royal Garrison Artillery but had to be discharged due to ill health.

Ayton arrived in Stirling for the Victory Tournament having given up his post as club professional at Rye and returned to St Andrews to give lessons. The tournament was played in late February and conditions were not ideal, but despite the rheumatism that plagued Ayton throughout his career, he achieved two solid rounds of 71 and 73 that were enough to beat Ben Sayers Jr into second place, three shots adrift.

Having won, Ayton felt that his future lay in the United States. It was not an easy decision to make for the patriotic Scot but, in his own words, 'there is very little doing in the winter months'. His departure, a few weeks later in March 1919, was much regretted by J. H. Taylor, who described his method as being that of 'a true son of St Andrews but sobered by a good dash of the English manner of playing. Driving a high, pushed-out and held-up ball and using a wooden putter to deadly effect, Ayton's game is most sound.' Taylor had good cause to know what he was talking about, having lost every time he played Laurie Ayton head-to-head! Britain's loss was America's gain as Ayton, taking up a new post at Evanston Club in Chicago, established an excellent reputation as a teacher and golf course architect.

With Ayton gone, Abe Mitchell set about staking his claim to the title of British number one with victory in the *Daily Mail* Professional Golfers Championship at St Andrews in June 1919. The tournament was back after a five-year hiatus, financed by Lord Northcliffe with a top prize of £100 with gold, silver and bronze medals for first, second and third places, and the field was open to the top 60 finishers in the 1914 Open Championship. With Mitchell and Duncan tying on a 4-round total of 312, it was decided that the best score in the Eden competition the next day would decide the winner of what amounted to an unofficial British Open. Scoring 77 to Duncan's 79, Mitchell was immediately installed as hot favourite to win the Open at Deal in 1920. Sadly for the man who went on to become Sam Ryder's personal coach, he led at the halfway stage only to have Duncan come from 13 strokes back, to steal the contest. It was a devastating blow from which Mitchell would never recover, and while he would continue to win 'minor' events throughout his career, he was never to capture the Open title he desperately craved.

While the professional game in Britain struggled on manfully in the immediate post-war years, a golfing revolution was taking place in the United States. Inspired by the huge public support they had received over the past two years of exhibition matches, by 1919 top American golfers were eager to test themselves against each other in serious competition now that the US Open, US Amateur and PGA Championship were back.

Golf Links and Pavilion, Honor Oak Park

Honor Oak Park golf course in South London was one of several not to survive the end of World War One.

Walter Hagen showed he had lost little of his competitive edge when, in June, he saw off a strong field to win the first post-war US Open, played in difficult conditions at Brae Burn Country Club in West Newton, Massachusetts. Hagen was expected to dominate the rest of the season but found himself playing second fiddle to his old rival Jim Barnes. Winning the Western Open in July, the lanky Cornishman then beat Fred McCloud 6&5 in the final of the PGA Championship at Engineers CC, New York, in September. Winner of the inaugural event in 1916, Barnes still retains the record for holding the Wanamaker trophy for the longest period.

In the amateur game there was also a wealth of dynamic young talent waiting in the wings, including future US Amateur Champions like Jesse Guilford, Jess Sweetser, George Von Elm and of course the greatest of them all, Robert T. Jones Jr. Improving in leaps and bounds, the former 'Dixie Boy' bettered the 4-round scoring record at the Canadian Open at Hamilton GC, finishing runner-up to J. Douglas Edgar, in July 1919. In August he lost 5&4 to hometown

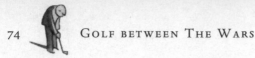

favourite S. Davidson Herron, in the final of the US Amateur at Oakmont. Jones was angry and upset; but finishing second was not a habit the 17-year-old Georgian would pick up during his meteoric rise to the top.

Of course it was not only the men who were showing promise. Fulfilling the potential she had shown as a teenager playing alongside Bobby Jones, Alexa Stirling added the US Women's Amateur Championship in 1919 and 1920 to the one she had won in 1916, paving the way for future Curtis Cup stars like Marion Hollins, Glenna Collett and Dorothy Campbell-Hurd. The growing threat to British golf's pre-war dominance was obvious, in both the women's game and the men's. While professionals and amateurs alike had continued playing, the war had stopped American golfers taking on their British cousins overseas. Now all they wanted was a crack at the top British stars to see how they measured up.

For players like Bobby Jones, Harry Vardon had been the benchmark against which any truly great player must measure himself. A brilliant competitor, Vardon had played just twice in the US Open —winner in 1900 and joint runner-up to Francis Ouimet in 1913. His brilliance had become legend and while his career was effectively over by the time the American invaders arrived in the early 1920s, the possibility of winning the British Open or British Amateur Championships was too exciting to contemplate for Jones and the rest.

As for the British, the thought that a 'Yank' could walk off with one of the game's most glittering prizes was too horrible to imagine. But they had not only George Duncan and Abe Mitchell to defend their honour but quality amateurs in Roger Wethered and Cyril Tolley. For a while it seemed to work; Duncan won the 1920 Open at Deal and Tolley, who had spent 13 months in a German prisoner-of-war camp, captured the Amateur Championship the same year. Yet, talented as they obviously were, they would prove no match for the American Armada who arrived in Britain to compete in the Open and Amateur Championships over the next decade or more. The

MINISTRY **MF** OF FOOD

RATION BOOK

(GENERAL) **1944-45**

Surname....*Tolley*....

Other Names....*Cyril James Hastings*....

Address....*Pommern Lodge*....
(as on Identity Card)

Paskby Rd Eastbourne....

N. N.
M.F.

NATIONAL REGISTRATION NUMBER *EHA. 1904 328*

R.B.1 7 GENERAL

FOOD OFFICE CODE No. **G**

S.E. 25

EASTBOURNE.

Serial No. of Ration Book

CM 658590

IF FOUND RETURN TO ANY FOOD OFFICE

23 JUN 1945

The World War II ration book of Cyril Tolley, British Amateur
champion in 1920, who had previously spent 13 months during the
Great War in a German prisoner-of-war camp.

record books show the mauling British golfers got at the hands
of players now living in America: from Jock Hutchison's play-
off victory over Roger Wethered at St Andrews in 1921, to
Densmore Shute's victory over the same course in 1933,
American golfers would capture 12 out of 13 British Open

Championships. With Bobby Jones coming into his prime and Walter Hagen as indomitable as ever, they won 7 titles between them, culminating in Jones's legendary 'Grand Slam' of British and American Open and Amateur Championships in 1930. With Jim Barnes (1925) Tommy Armour (1931) and Gene Sarazen (1932) sweeping up behind them, British golf, so dominant in the pre-war years, struggled hard to recover.

Not that America got off completely unscathed. In 1923 there had been 1903 golf courses in the United States, rising to 5648 by 1929. Then, as the Depression took hold in the early 1930s, nearly a million golfers—about 1 in 5 —gave up the game completely. Meanwhile, in Britain, during the 1930s golf remained the exclusive preserve of the rich. With a well-deserved reputation for snobbery and elitism, well-heeled golfers from London and the Home Counties saw golf club membership as a privilege to be jealously guarded. From 1920 to 1939 the working class was only allowed through the gates in the form of caddies, groundsmen or clubhouse servants. Typically, the club pro was tolerated out on the course or on the practice tee where he gave lessons, but was considered too low on the social scale to enter the clubhouse for a post-round drink. Like all club servants he was expected to know his place, and should he ever make the unpardonable mistake of calling a member by his first name, he would be hauled up before the committee to be given a thorough dressing down. (During one particular exhibition match, even six-time British Open champion Harry Vardon was asked to eat outside while the members repaired to the clubhouse for lunch!)

Change was slow but a huge blow was struck in 1920 when Ted Ray, professional at Oxhey Golf Club in Hertfordshire, was elected an honorary member to commemorate his historic victory in the US Open at Toledo earlier the same year. Even though he was a popular and highly respected figure in British golf, his appointment caused great controversy as middle-class golfers considered the implications of such a bold move. Then, when it finally dawned on them that hordes of

R.R.F Nº 2.Sᵗᵈ GOLF TEAM. 1924

working-class golfers had not besieged them with applications for membership, private clubs actually began to see the benefit of honouring their own star player in this way. Not surprisingly, South Herts Golf Club at nearby Totteridge quickly followed suit, making Harry Vardon an honorary member; as did Royal North Devon (J. H. Taylor) and Walton Heath (James Braid) in the years to come.

As the social barriers slowly began to crumble, it was suggested that professionals competing in the 1925 British Open at Prestwick might be allowed to change *inside* the clubhouse. Not surprisingly this too met with considerable opposition, but a compromise was reached: the players were permitted to use the changing rooms but not allowed in the members' bar. (Perhaps they recalled the example set at Deal in 1920 by Walter Hagen who, after being banned from using the clubhouse to change his shoes, turned up in a chauffeur-driven Rolls Royce and changed them in the car park!)

Despite the groundbreaking decision to allow them within the confines of the clubhouse, professionals were still critical of the arrangement and demanded better conditions at future Open Championships. Firmly putting the ball back in the court of golf's ruling body, representatives of the Royal and Ancient Golf Club met with the Professional Golfers Association and promised to review the matter. The following year at Royal Lytham and St Annes, players were allowed inside the clubhouse for the first time as 'temporary members'.

The diplomatic handling of this particularly sensitive issue by the PGA (formed in 1901 to protect the interests and welfare of its members) helped to establish a good working relationship with the R&A. In 1927, this 'amicable working arrangement' also helped when it came to the hugely contentious issue of legalising steel-shafted clubs in Britain in the wake of the US Golf Association's decision to legalise them in the United States.

The PGA also played a significant role in the promotion of golf up to the outbreak of war in 1939. While the R&A continued to organise the British Open and Amateur Championships, the PGA strove to fund a number of much smaller professional events based on the 'circuit' of tournaments that had proved so successful in the United States. And while funding such tournaments often proved problematic for the cash-strapped Association, events like the popular *News of the World* Championship continued to attract large crowds by pitching some of the biggest names head-to-head. Because positive publicity was considered essential to the success of such events, journalists were specially invited to cover tournaments from the mid-1920s onward, with a tented area set aside from which they could type their reports. Magazines like *Golf Illustrated* and *Golf Monthly*, and newspapers like the *Daily Telegraph* and *The Times* all covered golf in detail and made many of the players household names.

By the end of the 1930s, interest in golf rivalled the 'boom' years around the turn of the century. As the Ryder Cup had shown, Britain had golfers in the dashing young Henry Cotton, Dick Burton, Reg Whitcombe and Alfred Perry to rival the very best the United States had to offer. And while players like Gene Sarazen, Denny Shute and Walter Hagen no longer made the long sea journey to play in the British Open, hopes were high that the 1940s would reveal an even greater depth of home talent.

Unfortunately this was not to be, as the next decade saw little but blood, pain and sorrow for millions all over the world.

Three-times British Open champion Willie Park Jr left for the USA in March 1916 to pursue his golf-course designing business. The newspapers made a point of saying that he was over military age at the time.

Given special dispensation to play by the Army, George Duncan and his fellow professional Sid Ball took on Harry Vardon and J. H. Taylor in Manchester in 1917 on behalf of the Red Cross Hospital Fund. Duncan, an aeroplane rigger in the Royal Flying Corps and Ball, a corporal, played brilliantly and won the 36-hole foursomes match by 10&8. In fact they played so well that a wealthy American businessman offered them a 3-month exhibition tour of the USA after the war.

CHAPTER X

Golf in the Third Reich
1934 to 1945

IN THE 5 YEARS leading up to the start of World War II
ambitious plans were put in place to transform Nazi
Germany into a nation of elite golfers. The first hint came in
February 1934 when *The Times* published an official press state-
ment from the German Minister for Tourism in Wiesbaden.
He outlined ambitious plans to popularise golf in the fledgling
Reich Republic, describing how low-cost equipment would be
available for everyone, along with subsidised green fees on the
dozens of new golf courses that would be built, and hoping
that within 5 years German golfers would be challenging
golf's top prizes – including the British Open. Failure was not
a consideration. After all, the plan had the personal backing of
the Reich Führer himself – Adolf Hitler.

In the new Reich Republic all aspects of daily life were
being assessed for propaganda value, and sport was considered an important tool. Within months of the National
Socialists coming to power in 1933, new legislation was enact-
ed bringing 23 individual sports under control of central government. In the 1920s golf had been the preserve of the moneyed class in Germany, but the new plans proposed to bring it
within reach of the ordinary working-class man or woman.
Golf was also considered essential in attracting wealthy foreign visitors into Germany, and while Hamburg and Frankfurt
in the north already boasted a handful of top-quality courses
it was thought that many more would be needed over the

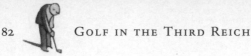

coming years. In a cynical attempt to exploit the game's reputation for sportsmanship and fair play, a publicity-grabbing
golf tournament was scheduled to follow the 1936 Olympic
Games in Berlin. It would be there that the Nazis hoped to
showcase Germany as a golfing nation.

Responsibility for turning Germans into golfers fell on
loyal party member Karl Henkell, who boasted strong political connections. Born on 14 April 1888, he was a member of
the renowned Wiesbadener Champagne-making family. By
the 1930s he was editor of the *Deutsche Golf Zeitung* (German
Golf News); his knowledge of international golf was unri-
valled. His appointment in January 1934 as *Führer des Deutschen
Golf-Verbandes* came as no surprise.

Henkell was described by *The American Golfer* magazine as
'an athletically-built, ruddy-faced gentleman, whose appearance belies his fifty odd years'. As former secretary of
Herzoglicher GC, Henkell knew exactly what it took to run a
successful club. Consequently his first action was to bring all
golf courses under the central control of the DGV (German
Golf Federation). From there he appointed every secretary/
manager, but not before declaring that 'every golfer must
speak German' and forbidding them to use English terms like
'fairway, caddie, birdie, stymie and driver'. He then ordered that
the swastika should be clearly visible in front of the clubhouse,
and under no circumstances should it be smaller than the club
flag! (Curiously, golf in Germany would still be played under
the rules of the Royal and Ancient Golf Club of St Andrews.)

That was just the beginning. By June 1934, Henkell had
scheduled a regular series of tournaments in which talented
young golfers could experience the cut and thrust of competition. A month later, he slashed the cost of membership to all
42 golf clubs in Germany from an average of 80 Reichsmarks
to just 2. Then, to encourage youngsters to take up the game,
he reduced it to 1 RM for anyone aged 18 and under.

To help pay for his ambitious plans, he persuaded the
Government to tax every German citizen 3 RM per annum

A very rare photograph of Karl Henkell, leader of the
Deutsches Golf-Verbandes, *meeting Bobby Jones, in Atlanta,*
Georgia in March 1936.

starting in September 1935. This *Golf Steuer* (golf tax) helped
provide free clubs and balls for those juniors not able to afford
them. It also paid the tuition fees of any talented German who
had shown promise during the previous year. As with everything in the Reich Republic, progress was swift: within 2 years
of Henkell's taking up his post, 13 new golf courses had been
built of which 10 were funded entirely by the state. With plans
to build at least 500 more by 1960, land was made available
near major cities like Berlin and Hamburg in the north and
Munich in the south. Finance was even made available for
research into green-keeping techniques, the results of which
would greatly benefit Britain and America in the period immediately after the war.

    Now that competitive golf was considered a high priority,
established courses at Cologne, Bad Salzbrunn, Berlin-
Wannsee, Baden-Baden, Bad Ems, Frankfurt-am-Main and
Hamburg-Falkenstein were all upgraded to championship
standard. With the majority now receiving generous govern-

Front cover of a promotional brochure extolling the pleasures of playing golf in pre-war Nazi Germany.

ment subsidies to offset the expense of offering low-cost membership, the facilities on offer began to match those found in the United States. Berlin Wannsee Golf and Country Club, set in the Grunewald Forest just outside the capital, boasted an impressive 5335-yard course, a 9-hole practice layout, and 4 teaching professionals including British Ryder Cup player Percy Alliss.

With new and better golf courses available, the Reich Committee for Tourism portrayed Germany as the ideal golfing destination for foreign visitors. Hoping to enforce that idea, Henkell arrived in the United States in March 1936 with a 30-strong delegation including 5 golf club presidents.

In a 6-week trip they travelled extensively from New York to Los Angeles, visiting courses in places like Pinehurst, Palm Beach, Atlanta and Brookline. Interest in the newly revitalised Germany was running high and they were treated as honoured guests, despite many people calling for an American boycott of the Berlin Games because of the Nazi regime's anti-Semitic leanings.

Describing golf as 'a decisive way out of despondency' and 'a game that makes us mentally healthy', the charismatic

Henkell gave interview after interview about the golfing boom in Germany. Claiming much of the credit, he offered an interesting insight into how things were done in Nazi Germany. Speaking in New York he said:

> We have today in Germany 55 well-organised clubs with a membership of approximately 5500. There is no German equivalent of the USGA or St Andrews, that is to say, no representative committee of players supervising the game. One might say that I constitute the German Golf Association. From my office in Wiesbaden, every activity pertaining to German Golf is conducted. There are no committees to be consulted or argued with. As a result, it is remarkably simple to get things done . . .

The New York Times published an article declaring that golf was now the national sport of Germany, while legendary sports writer Grantland Rice maintained that Germans were ideally suited to the rigours of tournament golf because 'it was a sport that required exactly the type of thoroughness that German people are famous for'.

Another, less publicised, reason behind Henkell's trip to the United States was his attempt to persuade top American players like Walter Hagen, Gene Sarazen and especially Bobby Jones to compete in his post-Olympic golf tournament at the end of August. Desperate to add these stars to the mainly amateur event, he lobbied relentlessly, even making a special trip to Atlanta to see Jones in person, but despite his offer to pay First Class travel expenses he failed to persuade anyone of note to travel to Germany.

The tournament was scheduled for the end of August and played in Baden-Baden; first prize was a brass salver inlaid with semi-precious stones. After 3 days of competition, England and Germany met in the final with the promise that should the home pair win, the Reich Führer himself would arrive and present the trophy. This was considered a great honour for Henkell, so he must have been distraught when the English pair defeated the home favourites. Adolf Hitler – who less than a week earlier had refused to present black American athlete Jesse Owens with his Olympic gold medal – withdrew immediately, leaving an embarrassed Foreign Minister Von Ribbentrop to present the trophy.

This incident proved to be the beginning of the end for Henkell's golfing ambitions. His plans might have survived despite Hitler's changeable nature, but within weeks of the Berlin tournament an even more severe blow was struck. In December 1936, in the wake of the Wallis Simpson affair, King Edward VIII became the first British monarch to abdicate his throne. As Prince of Wales, Edward had played golf in Germany on a number of occasions, often as the personal guest of Hitler. Counting on his support in any future negotiations with England, the German leader had favoured the sport of golf precisely because it was the favourite pastime of the English king.

Shortly after Edward VIII signed the Instrument of Abdication on 9 December, Hitler telephoned Von Ribbentrop in England to inform him that 'Now that the King has been dethroned, there is certainly no other person in England who is ready to play with us.' While he was not actually talking about golf, he might well have been. Hitler had lost his greatest pawn and from that moment any vague interest he had in the Royal and Ancient Game died. The Nazi regime's love affair with golf was over – but in any case the mask of civilisation had been slipping for some time. In 1933, the executive committee of the German Golf Federation had banned Jews from being involved in the day-to-day running of any club. Three years later in 1936, it decreed that no Jew could play golf on any course controlled by the DGV, which by this time included Austria, Bohemia and Luxembourg.

Without his leader's support, Henkell struggled hard to keep his department intact. As the tide of war turned against the Fatherland he continued to implement his original plan

*As the Prince of Wales, King Edward VIII had played golf in Nazi
Germany, even as the guest of Adolf Hitler.*

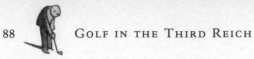

of bringing golf to the people, but it was proving virtually impossible without government finance which had all but dried up by 1941. With tractors and other machinery now requisitioned for the war effort the DGV annual report stated that 'each German golfer knows that our sport is in a particularly difficult position at this time'.

Describing the struggle of many German courses to survive, Henkell highlighted Kitzeburg Golf Club in Keil where retired members had been forced to take over green-keeping duties. Showing how social barriers had broken down, he recalled seeing 'four shabbily-dressed gentlemen happily cutting the greens – two admirals, a bank director and the Club Secretary'.

To his credit, the DGV managed to survive long into the war years and continued to arrange free golf for recovering servicemen. Describing Hamburg Golf Club as 'an oasis in the ruins of a sinking city', Karl Henkell made his last declaration in January 1944: 'We [Germans] must act in consciousness that all kinds of sport, thereby our golf, are regarded of less importance in this time of war...' A man of obvious integrity, he died on 10 February 1944 after a bombing raid over Wiesbaden.

His words proved true: the events of the war far overshadowed anything as trivial as sport. In the aftermath of World War II, the Allies dissolved all German government departments and sporting organisations including the DGV. With the Russian Army occupying the entire east of the country, only 22 golf courses survived the destruction. Not until 1965 would the total of German golf courses match pre-war figures.

Today, the reunified German Republic has almost 300 golf courses with many more in the planning stage. While the 'nation of golfers' envisaged by Henkell back in 1934 is still a long way off, at least it is moving in the right direction.

CHAPTER XI

World War II
Golf on the Home Front

W HEN WAR BROKE OUT in 1939, the British Government did not wait long before ordering golf to play its part in 'Keeping Adolf at Bay'.

A letter was sent to every club secretary, decreeing that obstructions must be placed on any flat ground that might serve as a landing strip for enemy aircraft. All over the country concrete pipes about 5 feet in length and filled with waste clinker were placed at 50-yard intervals, with a free drop given for any ball landing within a few feet. For any golfer unfortunate to actually hit one and bounce into the rough or sand, this was deemed 'rub of the green' and, along with other everyday obstacles like bomb craters, minefields and the occasional unexploded 44-millimetre shell, soon made golf a game to set the blood racing in new and unfamiliar ways. At Royal Liverpool, home to the 1936 British Open, golf was suspended for the duration with concrete and wooden posts sunk into the fairways to stop enemy gliders landing.

Typical of the war-affected courses was Rye in Kent. With each green surrounded by post and wire to keep grazing sheep at bay, members also had to contend with pillboxes, searchlight towers and machine-gun nests after a local Battle Unit commandeered the 5th and 6th fairways as a target range using live ammunition. It is probably due to what Winston Churchill described as the 'Bulldog Spirit' of these dedicated members that a course still exists at Rye. The dangers of play-

*Two groundsmen with their brooms surveying the wreckage of a
Heinkel He III bomber crashed and burned out on Blashington
Golf Course in Seaford, Sussex.*

ing golf in such wartime conditions were obvious. As late as
1944, Lieutenant R. H. Pilman of the Royal Armoured Corps
was killed instantly at Rye after attempting to retrieve his ball
from a wired-off minefield next to the course during an
impromptu fourball match.

Further north up the Kent coast at Sandwich, Prince's
Golf Club faced similar problems. Taken over by the army as
a practice firing range, it would be barely recognisable after
the war. Over at the West Kent club near Orpington, on the
edge of Greater London, anti-aircraft gun emplacements were
built on the links, leading to irreparable damage to the course.
German bombing raids on London saw the clubhouse also
wrecked. The whole of the South Coast was deemed a
'strategically important' area by the Government, and members of many clubs in the region were given the option of
playing their golf inland. Most were reluctant to leave. Many
clubhouses were determined to remain open and, despite a

number being targeted by enemy aircraft, the only major loss of life came at Ealing Golf Club in west London, where 5 golfers were killed in a bombing raid in February 1941.

Another London club that suffered badly was historic Royal Blackheath, a flying bomb in 1944 doing considerable damage to its Georgian clubhouse. But this was almost nothing compared to the fate of the golf clubs at Clapham Common and Tooting Bec: both were bombed so badly that they were unable to reopen after the war and public parks are all that remains. The better-known English clubs like Walton Heath and Sunningdale remained open for regular bridge sessions even though both their courses were closed for long periods of the war. At Woking, the Army stuck to a long-standing agreement brokered during World War I not to carry out manoeuvres on the course. (In a ploy worthy of Rommel, the committee continued their tradition of making all high-ranking officers honorary members.)

At Richmond Park near London, members were determined to play golf despite air raids and threat of invasion as shown by the set of temporary rules drawn up in 1941:

1. *Players are asked to collect the bomb and shrapnel splinters to save these causing damage to the mowing machines.*
2. *In competitions, during gunfire or while bombs are falling, players may take shelter without penalty or ceasing play.*
3. *The position of known delayed-action bombs are marked with red flags at a reasonable, but not guaranteed, safe distance therefrom.*
4. *Shrapnel or bomb splinters on the fairways, or in bunkers, within a club's length of the ball, may be moved without penalty, and no penalty shall be incurred if a ball is thereby caused to move accidentally.*
5. *A ball moved by enemy action may be replaced, or if lost or destroyed, a ball may be dropped not nearer the hole without penalty.*
6. *A ball lying in a crater may be lifted and dropped not*

nearer the hole, preserving the line to the hole, without penalty.

7. *A player whose stroke is affected by a simultaneous explosion of a bomb may play another ball. Penalty one stroke.*

With the Home Guard using its clubhouse as their HQ, Hoylake on the Wirral opened up its plush changing rooms to a local Searchlight Detachment – but only between 7.00 and 9.30 in the morning. 'After all,' wrote a disgruntled member in the *Liverpool Standard*, 'There was no reason for letting standards slip – even in wartime!'

Out on the Wirral, Wirral Ladies' Club must have felt far enough away from Liverpool not to be targeted by Hitler's bombers, and agreed to store 300 sets of clubs, records and trophies on behalf of bombed-out Bromborough Golf Club. But in 1942 Wirral Ladies were bombed, and lost everything.

Up on the Lancashire Coast, Royal Lytham and St Annes fared rather better. Retaining a skeleton green staff, the club carried on much as usual – members even invited local RAF officers to play their monthly medal competitions. In 1943, the invitation was extended to American Air Force personnel at nearby Warton Airfield. Any American who had no clubs was loaned a set that belonged to a member who was stationed overseas or presently incarcerated in a German prisoner-of-war camp! One American later recalled the unusual welcome that awaited them from club pro Tom Fernie when they turned up at Royal Lytham to play free of charge: '[He] would question us about our scores and proffer sets of first-class clubs to those he deemed worthy of them.'

In Scotland the game continued despite fenced-off greens and an abundance of grazing sheep. Dunbar Golf Club in particular, located beneath the Lammermuir Hills, had had a long time to get used to the incursions of war, boasting a military history as long as its golfing one. Oliver Cromwell's Parliamentary army camped there shortly before the battle of

*Golfers in Leeds dig for victory by turning the city's golf
course into vegetable allotments.*

Dunbar in 1650. In 1802, another force mustered on the links in
preparation for an expected invasion by Napoleon. Another
140 years on, and trenches were dug and mines laid on the
course to defend the Scottish coastline against a German landing. Then, as the threat of invasion receded, the club pre-
served its precious links by persuading the Ministry of
Agriculture that it was an ideal place to graze sheep rather
than growing crops. It is a sobering thought that some of the
most famous links courses in Scotland probably owed their
survival to the sandy soil that makes them so unique. At a
time when countless other golf courses throughout Britain,
especially those inland, were being ploughed under to provide
food for the war effort, the large majority of links were
deemed unsuitable because of the acidity of their soil.

At St Andrews, both Winston Churchill and General
Eisenhower were occasional visitors but declined any offer to
play the threadbare links. At North Berwick, the 12th and 13th
fairways were fenced off in 1941 and a minefield laid, with the

*An amphibian tank exercise in February 1943 on a golf course
near a Combined Operations Training Centre at Dundonald Camp
in Scotland.*

appropriate 'out-of-bounds' signs in good view. At nearby
Muirfield, deep trenches were dug and huge concrete blocks
laid all over the course as tank traps (some of these massive
concrete 'tank-stoppers' can still be seen down the coast at the
Gullane club), but the Honourable Company of Edinburgh
Golfers strenuously opposed a proposal for laying a minefield
over their hallowed turf! They won that battle, but later in the
war the course had become so overgrown with thistles that 90
German POWs were drafted in to repair the damage.

In August 1940, a large bomb was dropped on Stonehaven
Golf Course by a German aircraft fleeing home after an air
raid on nearby Aberdeen. The crater it left between the first
and second fairways – a hazard to this day – has long been
known locally as 'Hitler's bunker'. At Carnoustie, caddies
were under strict orders to carry a gas mask for them *and* one
for their employer as a precaution against German attack. In
1941, Turnberry on the West Coast was requisitioned as an air
base for trainee fliers learning how to fire aerial torpedoes. A
long runway was driven across both the Arran and Ailsa courses with another one bisecting it, leaving the links unrecognis-

able from peacetime. So drastic was the damage that there was serious doubt as to whether the courses could be revived after the war. Visitors can still see traces of the old runways, and pillboxes and gun emplacements remain in place. As well as the Beaufighters used for torpedo training, the aerodrome was home to long-range American-built Liberator heavy bombers used for anti--submarine sorties and convoy patrols across the Atlantic. The RAF requisitioned the famous hotel too, and turned it into a hospital. As well they might, because many learner pilots crashed in the hazardous terrain.

Over in Northern Ireland Ormeau Park Golf Club was pressed into service as a temporary holding pen for hundreds of sheep prior to their being herded into an abattoir for slaughter and then shipped from the docks for shipment to England as lamb. The committee protested to the Government about the 'mess' left on the greens and was told by the local council that if it complained again, the course would be closed for good!

Another viable target for wartime agriculture was Wentworth in Surrey. The club had been requisitioned by the Army as a possible wartime HQ, and prior to the war a massive bunker and network of tunnels had been constructed under the clubhouse, with bomb-proof concrete walls 6 feet thick and an escape tunnel emerging near the 18th green on the East Course. By the end of the 1930s, with such uncertainty hanging over its golfing future, the club had gone into receivership. The course was now in poor condition, but though officers working at Wentworth were entitled to play it they were not allowed to do so for free. Honorary membership cost them 1 shilling, and a round on the East Course 3 pennies. The West Course had longer, flatter fairways, and to prevent enemy planes landing there it was allowed to grow wild. After the war, it was earmarked for food storage in the event of a nuclear attack on the capital.

Finding a course in playable condition was not the only formidable hazard for the wartime golfer. With fuel severely

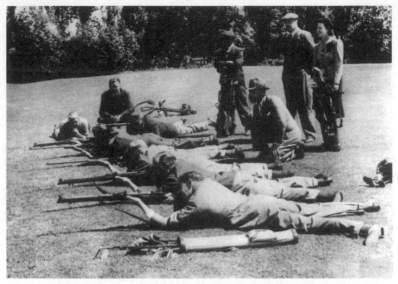

*Golfers in Kent were told to carry guns in case
German paratroopers landed.*

rationed, signposts unreliable and the wartime train service
infrequent at best, reaching the course at all could prove difficult enough. Tongue-in-cheek tips from *Golf Monthly* on how
to play golf in a gas mask and tin hat hint at what a game
would have been like – but the would-be golfer probably
lacked the implements to play at all, as the production of golf
equipment had been halted for the duration and golf balls
were now scarce and valuable.

Elsewhere in the British Commonwealth, playing conditions were no better. In Australia all professional events were
cancelled from an early stage of the war; some clubs, such as
Royal Melbourne, played a monthly medal in aid of war relief.
On the Indian subcontinent, Royal Calcutta Golf Club, having
dutifully rendered its course unusable to enemy aircraft, contributed 50,000 rupees to the East India Fund to buy a Spitfire.
Then as refugees started pouring in from Burma in 1943, those
who played golf (including former members of Rangoon Golf
Club) were offered temporary membership. Here, too, petrol

rationing was a constant problem and golf balls were in short supply: members were allowed to buy just 1 every 2 months.

From 1940 onward, production of golf balls ceased, leaving players with nothing but pre-war stock, remoulds and in some cases wooden balls. (During the 1940 US Open, there were rumours in Britain that American professionals were using golf balls with magnetic cores that could travel unheard-of distances!) At Pulborough in East Sussex, astonished visitors were often handed a pair of Wellington boots and invited to find themselves a golf ball in the pond on the 5th before teeing off! Rarely have players been as thorough about marking their golf balls in the rough as during that period.

With pro shop sales at an all-time low, the British PGA took pity on their dwindling band of members by reducing their annual subscription to 10 shillings for full pro's and 5 shillings for assistants, and offering a full exemption for any member serving in the Armed Forces – and there were many of these. Following in the footsteps of the famed Niblick Brigade in World War I, the PGA set an example for the 1939-45 conflict with over 664 pro's enlisting in the armed forces — well over half the total membership at the time. While only a handful had returned from the Great War, news was far better for the professional ranks two decades later with only 27 killed, 27 taken prisoner and another 23 invalided out.

For British tournament pro's the war years were an era of frustration, worsened by the fact that whereas the British Open lost 6 years (1940-45) the US Open lost only 4 (1942-45), the US Masters 3 (1943-45) and the US PGA just 1 (1943). While their American counterparts were playing for $117,000 in prize money in 1940 alone, golfers like Reg Whitcombe, British Open champion in 1938, had a potentially brilliant career cruelly interrupted by the war. Along with Henry Cotton (Army captain), Max Faulkner (Commando trainer) and Charlie Ward (RAF ground crew), other hugely talented players like Sam King, Dick Burton and Arthur Lacey would all struggle after the war to regain their former game. In the

Left *Max Faulkner, British Open Champion in 1951,
in his wartime RAF uniform;* right *Henry Cotton, who served
as an Army captain.*

words of Faulkner, 1951 British Open champion, 'It was not just the six years I lost because of the war, it was the six years it took getting my game in shape afterwards.'

The Ryder Cup also fell victim to the war. After the USA defeated Great Britain and Ireland at Southport and Ainsdale in 1937, Walter Hagen was chosen to reprise his role as American playing captain at Ponte Vedra, Florida in the 1939 event, scheduled for November. PGA Secretary R. C. T. Roe reluctantly cabled the American PGA to announce that the match would have to be cancelled due to the outbreak of war in Europe.

With both teams already in place, it was decided to honour them by announcing their names in the press as if the match was going ahead. (A medal was also struck by the US PGA and given to each American team member.) For the USA it was Hagen, Ralph Guldahl, Dick Metz, Harold McSpaden,

*A Royal Navy rating on leave in Cairo in May 1943 tees off
at the Gezira Sporting Club's golf course.*

Byron Nelson, Vic Ghezzi, Henry Picard, Horton Smith, Jimmy Hines and Sam Snead. With two places left open for late qualifiers, the Great Britain and Ireland side was Henry Cotton (captain), Dick Burton, Sam King, Jimmy Adams, Dai Rees, Alf Padgham, Charles Whitcombe and Reg Whitcombe.

In 1941, a commemorative exhibition match, with the Ryder Cup trophy at stake, was held at Detroit Golf Club, pitting a team led by legendary amateur Bobby Jones against one led by the flamboyant professional Walter Hagen. Stars of the day like Hogan, Snead and Nelson played alongside old-timers like Tommy Armour, and almost $15,000 was raised for the United Service Organization. A similar event was planned for 1942 but with so many players away in the Armed Forces, it was a fairly low-key affair with Hagen and Gene Sarazen as honorary captains, at Oakland Hills Country Club.

When the war ended in 1945, plans were made to resume the biannual match a year later. Unfortunately, by that time many of British golf's top players were still completely out of practice and the British PGA decided to put off the match until 1947. But as the crushing 11-1 defeat for Britain in Portland,

After the cruiser HMS
Manchester *has been torpedoed*
in the Mediterranean in July 1941
while on convoy duty, a naval
officer is concerned to salvage
his golf clubs.

Oregon proved, even that was far too early.

Desperate to get the professional game under way as quickly as possible, Commander Roe and the PGA organised 5 tournaments in 1945. The most significant was The *Daily Mail* Victory Tournament at St Andrews in the autumn, often called the 'unofficial' or 'lost' Open, which attracted 172 entrants. Many competitors, including Lloyd Mangrum, turned up in uniform; and the winner, Charles H. Ward, was confined to barracks after returning to his RAF camp at Wallingfold a day late because the presentation made him miss his train!

This popular and well-attended tournament showed just how much the British public had missed top-quality competition. A year later, the R&A was given sole responsibility for organising the first 'official' British Open after the war. Again St Andrews was the venue, but this time there would be no home-grown winner for the crowds to cheer. Instead, Samuel Jackson Snead – who had caught his first glimpse of the Old Course from his railway carriage a few days earlier and mistaken it for a disused plot of land – won with a score of 290.

A new era in golf had begun.

CHAPTER XII

Golf and the Great Escape

No matter how harsh the conditions, golfers will always try to keep playing.

Inside the German prisoner-of-war camps of World War II many ingenious means of golfing were found, as servicemen battled the twin evils of boredom and lack of physical activity. With club heads made from scrap metal and balls fashioned from pine cones wrapped in old shoe leather and stitched with string from Red Cross parcels, a crude version of golf was possible – and for many, that was all that mattered.

While golf was played at a number of camps in Germany, the best-known was Stalag Luft III at Sagan. Scene of the legendary 'Great Escape' in March 1944, in which 76 Allied servicemen tunnelled out, it has now become part of World War II folklore. The camp was situated 100 miles southeast of Berlin, now in modern-day Poland, and was one of 6 operated by the Luftwaffe for captured British and American airmen. Opened in May 1942 under the command of Oberst (Colonel) Friedrich-Wilhelm von Lindeiner-Wildau, it was a model of civilised internment, covering a massive 59 acres and holding over 10,000 prisoners. A gym was built and areas were set aside for football and cricket, but prison was still prison and life could be grim.

Golf at Stalag Luft III started in a small way but quickly attracted a big following. Sidney Smith, a journalist from the *Daily Express*, received a wooden-shafted women's mashie (5-iron) via the Red Cross and began by hitting pebbles between

Three views of the golf course constructed in the exercise yard
at Stalag Luft III. In the bottom right picture it is Competition Day;
in the bottom-left picture the 'death zone' can be clearly seen
to the right of the green.

the huts. He was joined by Pat Ward-Thomas, later the golf correspondent of the *Guardian*, and the next stage was a private competition between the two men to see who would take the lowest number of shots to hit a tree-stump target. Growing ambitious, they would spend hours making more aerodynamic balls by covering pebbles or pine cones in tightly wrapped cloth. These would then be encased in leather and stitched shut, before being treated with black shoe-polish to keep them waterproof. Pat Ward-Thomas recalled the most popular material in his autobiography *Not Only Golf*: 'The man with rubber to spare or exchange was the golfer's friend. Prisoners were allowed quarterly clothing parcels from home, and many was the plea for gym shoes, air cushions, tobacco pouches and the like.'

As the equipment got better so did the golf course. Designed by Flight Lieutenant Danny O'Brien (a former Scottish schoolboy international) and Flight Lieutenant Percy Thomas, an 18-hole 'course' was constructed, with small sandy greens ('browns') and rusty tomato cans hammered into the hard ground as the cups. The holes ranged in distance between 50 and 70 yards, with each 'brown' surrounded by a nest of bunkers. (The Germans quickly intervened when a number of sand traps became deep enough to hide an escaping POW from the camp searchlights.) Not surprisingly, the antique mashie owned by Sid Smith, used as a putter, was suddenly in great demand. 'That little mashie must have hit several hundred thousand golf shots, often in the hands of strong, unskilled players,' recalled Ward-Thomas. 'That it survived was a rare tribute to the quality of the hickory.'

Preferred lies became the norm and though the longest 'hit' was only 70 yards, regular competitions were held and there was a huge amount of gambling on the outcome, using camp currency called 'lagergeld'. While the greens never wore out, footprints and other marks were a constant irritation to many golfers. The course was swept with a handmade string broom before play started and swept again by each passing group. Eventually it was decided to appoint a full-time 'brown' keeper named Tommy Biden, who was given the task of removing stones and smoothing the sand by hand each day – but the camp guards, with the possibility of tunnelling constantly on their minds, became concerned about the amount of 'contouring' going on.

The POWs committee persuaded the guards to let play continue, but the next problem was a series of complaints

Wing-Commander Douglas Bader, legless Battle of Britain fighter pilot and keen golfer, was a prisoner-of-war in Colditz Castle from 1942 to 1945.

about errant golf shots. The games area was used for baseball, football, and even ice hockey when rainwater froze over in winter, and the golf course had to fit around these, using whatever ground was available. The 6th hole, for example, was played over the kitchen hut and brought complaints from the German cooks who tired of hearing loud thuds as novice golfers 'thinned' their tee-shots. Another source of contention was the testing 18th, which used the camp water supply as a hazard! For fear of reprisals, the course was reduced to just 9 holes with a total yardage of 850 yards.

More and more people joined in the fun, and the only rule was that each POW had to make his own club and ball. By 1944, quite sophisticated equipment was being churned out and any spare bits and pieces discarded in the North Compound would be snaffled up before they hit the ground. Usable club heads were the greatest challenge, and many were made from melted-down silver cigarette paper ingeniously cast in a sand mould in the ground. Then, as golf became more popular, unusable lead water-jugs were melted down and shaped into club heads, far less fragile than the earlier models. Branches were taken from the trees for use as shafts.

Another problem was the camp perimeter fence. With a number of holes situated near a 10-yard strip of land between the inner and outer fences, it was inevitable that many balls would land inside this so-called 'death zone'. A warning barrier known as a 'low rail' or 'trip wire' marked this definitely out-of-bounds area, and POWs were expected to wait for a guard who would retrieve the ball for them. Inevitably, this meant a long delay and the temptation to retrieve an errant ball that had taken hours to make proved too tempting for some prisoners, who would literally risk their lives trying to get it back in play.

These attempts were likely to be construed as an escape attempt by the guards, who were entitled to shoot first and ask questions later. Even if the player survived, he would face 7 days in solitary confinement! With golf and football played all day during summer it was inevitable that balls should fly over the trip wire into this no-man's-land, but common sense finally prevailed. It was agreed that a white butcher's coat should be used by anyone stepping inside the 'death zone', as a sort of safe-conduct.

Then, in 1944, came the Great Escape, causing chaos throughout the area. Many of the POWs were captured within hours and retribution was not long in coming. Within a week of the mass escape all exercise privileges were suspended, with the Sagan course completely flattened by the German guards. This was a hard blow to those golfers too old or infirm to take part in the escape. The course was eventually rebuilt 6 months later, but in the spring of 1945 the camp was liberated by the Russians.

Donating a number of POW golf balls to the R&A many years later, Pat Ward-Thomas recalled wondering how anyone could miss such huge greens having played the tiny 'browns' at Stalag Luft III. 'Sadly,' he wrote, 'the illusion did not last long…'

"FIRST THING I WANT TO IMPRESS ON YOU MEN, IS THAT YOU AINT FREE TO COME AND GO AT WILL!"

CHAPTER XIII

Uncle Sam goes to War
1941 to 1946

AFTER THE JAPANESE ATTACK on Pearl Harbor on 7 December 1941, the United States of America officially entered World War II. Within weeks, the USGA had cancelled the US Open, the men and women's Amateur Championships and the National Public Links tournament. Under pressure to follow their example, PGA president Ed Dudley asked for official guidance as to whether or not they should continue holding professional tournaments. President Roosevelt's government replied that they should play fund-raising events for war charities such as the Red Cross and USO. War Commissioner Paul McNutt then eased everyone's fears by saying that golf should not be considered 'an unpatriotic diversion' in time of war, as professional sport could be used to raise public morale. War or no war, it seemed golf would carry on.

Another government appointee to have a significant impact on US golf was 1920 Olympic sculling champion John B. Kelly. Asked by FDR to head the 'Hale America' campaign*, the 53-year-old millionaire building contractor (and father of actress Grace Kelly) was given the task of getting 'America fit for war'. Appointed Assistant US Director of Civilian Defence in Charge of Physical Fitness in February 1942, he crisscrossed the country stressing the importance of physical exercise to

---

* Hale as in 'hale and hearty'

Jack Kelly, tasked by Roosevelt with getting 'America fit for war', suggested a series of golf tournaments on public holidays, with the money raised going to war relief.

the health of the nation. Outlining the vital role golf had in these troubled times, he suggested the USGA organise a series of tournaments on public holidays like Memorial Day, Independence Day and Labor Day, the profits going to war relief. In response to a speech he gave at Bellevue in May, asking golfers to donate any spare clubs and balls to soldiers on active service, the local Women's Golf Association collected over 1300 clubs and 140 bags! Wonderful publicity for the Hale America program – the Philadelphia *Inquirer* published a photograph of a smiling Jack Kelly perched on top of this veritable mountain of golf equipment.

The effect was immediate, with the Philadelphia PGA launching a scheme called 'Golf for the Armed Forces'. A threefold initiative, its purpose was to collect any unwanted golf clubs from pro shops; to offer enlisted men reduced access to golf courses in the Pennsylvania/Delaware/New Jersey area; and to organise charity golf matches and trick-shot exhibitions at local military installations.

Wartime also meant sacrifice, as American golfers quickly found. In those early months after Pearl Harbor, courses all over the country were asked to 'donate' one or two holes for growing food for the war effort. In a rush of patriotic fervour many did, but the biggest problem facing ordinary golfers was, as all over the world, a severe lack of golf balls. In January 1942 the Office of Price Administration ordered an 80 per cent

American GIs play their homemade crazy golf course at Bougainville
in New Guinea during the war in the Pacific.

reduction in ball production, causing an immediate stampede
to sporting goods shops to buy up any remaining stock. With
pro shops unable to supply their members, day-to-day golf in
the United States was under threat and despite imports of
many thousands of balls from Scotland from 1943 onward, the
situation soon reached crisis point. In November 1942, the
board of Gulph Mills near Philadelphia discussed the possibility of advancing cash to the club professional for buying extra
golf balls, most of whose stock 'had been placed in the vaults
of the Pennsylvania Company for safekeeping'.

Taking a lead in April 1943, the USGA donated 1000 balls
for distribution among the Army, Navy and Air Force. Having
cancelled the US Open at the outbreak of war, they must have
looked on in envy as the PGA maintained a reduced schedule
of tournaments well into 1942. But with many of its star
players enlisting in the Armed Forces, the PGA would face
difficulties of its own over the coming 12 months. Drafted into

Major Robert T. 'Bobby' Jones Jr in 1944, actively involved in the Normandy Landings.

the Navy in December 1941, Ed 'Porky' Oliver became the first 'name' player to join up, followed by Sam Snead, Lew Worsham, Jimmy Demaret and Herman Keiser the following year. Jim Turnesa, Clayton Heafner, Dutch Harrison, Jim Ferrier, Vic Ghezzi, Lloyd Mangrum, Ben Hogan and Horton Smith all joined the Army. Jimmy Thompson went into the Coast Guard, while Henry Ransom signed up for the Merchant Marine Corps.

Unlike many of their fellow pro's who spent their time playing golf and giving lessons to the top brass, Heafner, Ghezzi and Smith all saw action overseas while 1940 Masters winner Lloyd Mangrum earned four Battle Stars and two Purple Hearts, being wounded during the Battle of the Bulge. (A staff sergeant with the Third Army, he also participated in the D-Day landings before returning home in 1945.)

Another golfer who served with distinction during the war years was the legendary Robert T. Jones Jr. Desperate to enlist, the now 40-year-old father-of-three had a medical condition that barred him from active service; yet he managed to pull strings and get commissioned as an Army Air Force intelligence officer in 1942. After that he joined the personal staff of his friend General Eisenhower and was actively involved in the Normandy landings. Given the task of interviewing top-ranking German officers, he finally left the army with the exalted rank of lieutenant colonel two years later. (Typically, Eisenhower found an ideal retreat while based in London dur-

Ben Hogan wins the 1942 Hale America National Open at Ridgemoor,
the tournament held to replace that year's cancelled US Open.

ing the war – a 5-bedroom house named Telegraph Cottage, which backed onto the 13th hole at Coombe Hill Golf Club south of the capital.)

Back in America it was decided that a tournament should replace the cancelled US Open in June 1942. Taking the slot allocated to the Chicago Open, The Hale America National Open went ahead at Ridgemoor Country Club near Chicago. While the course was not up to National Open standards, it did offer the War Bond equivalent of $2000 for the winner (War Bond dollars were worth approximately 75 per cent of the real thing), along with a commemorative gold medal. The result was never in doubt after Ben Hogan's second round of 62 en route to a 17-under-par aggregate. Pushing Mike Turnesa and Jimmy Demaret into second, at least it helped ease the painful memory of his play-off defeat to Byron Nelson at the Masters in April.

A patriotic American and proud winner, Hogan always

claimed that his win in the Hale America tournament rated alongside any of his 4 US Open titles. He was already enlisted in the Army by the time Slammin' Sam Snead won the PGA Championship at Seaview in New Jersey 7 weeks later in August (Snead requested that his enlistment into the Navy be delayed by 10 days so he could compete); Lieutenant Hogan had enrolled in Officer Candidates School in July. The leading money-earner, with 6 victories and over $13,000 in official prize money, he was billeted with fellow star Horton Smith on the former grounds of Bayshore Country Club in Miami Beach, where the first fairway had been converted into a parade ground and obstacle course and even the camp marching song had a golf theme. Sung to the tune of 'Take me out to the Ball Game', it went:

> Off we go to the golf course.
> We ain't gonna play golf.
> Gone are the caddies around the place,
> Gone are the balls we once used to chase.
> For they've levelled off all the sand traps,
> Closed up the bar and grill,
> No, it's not for golf that we're out,
> It's a goddam drill.

Singing about golf would be the nearest Ben Hogan would get to a serious game for two years. One of America's best paid sportsmen in 1937, he was now pulling in just $50 a month in the Army Air Corps and would do so for the next two and a half years. Not that he was forgotten completely: when the Hale America National Open was renamed the Chicago Victory National Golf Championship in 1943, a letter was sent by the organisers 'requesting' that Hogan return the trophy! (The championship was played at Beverly CC and was won by New York Yankees right fielder turned pro golfer, Sam Byrd.)

With no official prize money listed by the PGA, just 3 tournaments were held in 1943, including the Knoxville Open in August where 18 pro's turned up to compete for 20 prizes – and even one of those got himself disqualified! Seizing this golden opportunity for any pro looking for his first and possibly only tournament victory, Steve Warga, an unknown airline radio operator, captured the Miami Open in December as the season faded from the memory. (The North and South tournament was also held that year but was restricted to golfers aged 38 years and over, and was won by World War I veteran Bobby Cruickshank.)

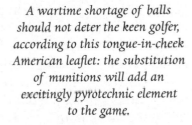

A wartime shortage of balls should not deter the keen golfer, according to this tongue-in-cheek American leaflet: the substitution of munitions will add an excitingly pyrotechnic element to the game.

Grassroots golf was also struggling hard to survive. In June 1943, the Chicago District Golf Association introduced its Dime-a-Round initiative, whereby golfers deposited a dime in a milk bottle before the start of each round. That was about all many could afford, and as memberships plummeted so did clubhouse revenue. Golf courses were now vulnerable to being requisitioned for the war effort, and even the Alister MacKenzie-designed Sharp Park in Pacifica, California was utilised as an internment camp for Japanese and German aliens later the same year.

Over in Pennsylvania, Glendale Country Club was commandeered by the US Housing Authority to build homes for defence workers. In 1943 the country club in Philadelphia gave up its Spring Mill course so that the US Army could test out new camouflage methods on the grass, then became concerned as its membership dropped alarmingly to 638 from a record 1349 in 1928. Olympia Fields in Illinois only survived because it sold off 2 of its 4 golf courses.

Early in the war Augusta National closed its course for the duration. Then in January 1943 it purchased 50 head of cattle, to provide fresh meat for those members who continued to use the clubhouse. Among those who followed this example was Baltusrol, which abandoned all thoughts of golf and went into the livestock business. With a nationwide shortage of fresh meat, the club even announced a small profit in November 1943 from the herd of cows and flock of sheep reared on its two courses.

By the start of 1944, the war against Germany and Japan had turned in the Allies' favour. People were in the mood for enjoyment, and watching top-class sport came high on the agenda. In cities like New York and Chicago huge crowds turned up as always to watch baseball matches and college football, but with major league teams manned by overweight veterans trading on their former reputations and inexperienced kids awaiting the draft, it was difficult to forget that all the best players were away fighting.

Golf was in the same situation. With many of its star players serving in the armed forces, the PGA struggled to organise just 3 events in 1943. Crowds were non-existent along with prize money, leaving most pro's to scratch a living by giving lessons in between playing War Bond matches. Like millions of ordinary club members, the biggest problem they faced was getting enough petrol. (One enterprising exception was the golfers of Farmingdale, Long Island, who rented a horse-drawn cart to transport them from the Long Island Rail Road station to the nearby golf course at Bethpage State Park.)

It was obvious to everyone that this was going to be a tough war.

CHAPTER XIV

Byron Nelson
and his Winning Streak

DESPERATE TO SHAKE OFF the effect of the last couple of years, the American PGA organised a schedule of 22 tournaments for 1944, including the first major championship in 2 years – the PGA at Spokane in August, backed with $20,000 from the Athletic Institute (an organisation formed by top sporting goods manufacturers). This was clearly a big financial risk, as players such as Hogan and Snead were still unavailable. However, the PGA held a couple of real aces in the shape of Byron Nelson and Harold 'Jug' McSpaden. Rejected by the Army for health reasons, they would single-handedly revive interest in golf over the next 12 months, earning the sobriquet 'the Gold Dust twins' by the amount of prize money they won.

John Byron Nelson Jr already had a formidable record by the time World War II put a halt to tournament golf in 1942. Born in Fort Worth, Texas, he had won the PGA Championship in 1940 and the US Masters in 1937 and 1942, as well as 23 other tournament victories. By any standards he was a great player, but there was something missing. A tall, rangy figure with a mechanical swing, he went about his business quietly and with very little fuss. While others hogged the limelight, he just picked up his cheque, said thank you and headed off for the next tournament. Lacking the charisma of Hogan or the country-boy charm of Snead, he played most of his career in the shadow of both and it was not until they had entered

Byron Nelson.

the Armed Forces that he really began to shine.

Like Craig Wood, who was judged unfit for military service because of a back injury sustained in a car crash many years earlier, 30-year-old Nelson was rejected by the Army after he was found to have haemophilia (a hereditary condition that prevents blood from clotting). A similar fate befell the combative, sunglass-wearing McSpaden, who suffered from asthma – though the Kansas-born player had refused to let illness affect his career, winning the Canadian Open in 1939 after finishing runner-up in the PGA Championship in 1937.

Though he was a workmanlike professional, 'Jug' (nicknamed for his prominent ears) would probably never have had the success he did had it not been for the war years. Granted extensive leaves of absence to take part in War Bond matches by his home club of Philadelphia, Jug, like Byron Nelson, spent the next 2 years trying to ignore the disapproving looks of those who wondered why such fit-looking men were not serving overseas. (Nelson later admitted to resigning from his post as club professional at Inverness after hearing that a number of members were unhappy about the money he was making from tournaments and exhibition matches.)

McSpaden explained his own attitude to the Philadelphia *Inquirer* on 28 April 1944: 'The Tour, I feel, not only will help

Horton Smith, left, in military uniform, with Henry Cotton.

the war effort, but also will stimulate interest in golf . . . Some of our best friends in service – Ben Hogan, Jimmy Demaret, Sam Snead, Jimmy Thomson, Lawson Little, Paul Runyan, Horton Smith – have asked us to play as much as we can in order to keep the game going for them.'

From 1942 to 1944 Nelson and McSpaden often teamed up with entertainers Bob Hope and Bing Crosby to play exhibition matches all over the country. Encouraging the link between golf and Hollywood, the PGA extolled the 'therapeutic value' of playing the game, citing health-giving properties like fresh air, exercise and good comradeship. (Money raised from the 1944 Chicago Victory National Golf Championship at Edgewater Golf Club enabled putting greens to be built at the Hines and Downey Veterans' Hospitals for the benefit of hos-

The 'Gold Dust Twins' in action: Harold 'Jug' McSpaden drives off, with Byron Nelson looking on

pitalised American soldiers.)

The previous 2 years had been a struggle for both McSpaden and Nelson and it came as a great relief when the PGA announced 18 events for 1944. This was an opportunity the 'Gold Dust Twins' would each grab with both hands, and they worked hard over the winter, Nelson on his chipping and McSpaden on his putting. The effort paid off, resulting in scores that would have been outstanding even in peacetime. Beginning the season in Los Angeles, McSpaden came out on top before finishing second to Nelson in San Francisco the following week. In the third tournament, at Phoenix, their budding rivalry was confirmed after Jug beat Byron in an 18-hole play-off, holing a 20-foot birdie putt on the penultimate green to win by a single shot. 'I think that's the happiest I ever saw him in golf,' wrote Nelson afterwards. 'Because the rest of the time, I just happened to be fortunate enough to sneak out on him one way or another.'

At the end of 10 events Nelson was 60 under par — McSpaden for the same tournaments was a remarkable 69 under! Despite that, McSpaden ended the season runner-up to Nelson who won 8 events (out of 23) compared with his 5. finishing no worse than sixth all season, the Texan won the War Bond equivalent of $38,000, smashing the money-earning record of $19,500 set by Sam Snead in 1938. His average score of 69.67 for 85 competitive rounds remained a record for years to come. And even though McSpaden fell away in the second half of the year due to poor putting, the high standard set by both men had captured the public imagination. 'If you were not born,' Jug often said to Byron, 'I'd be known as a good player...'

If golf fans thought Byron Nelson had played well in 1944, his performance the following season still stands out in the annals of golf history. From 11 March to 4 August 1945, he won every event he entered and achieved a never-to-be-equalled 11 consecutive victories. His year ended with a record 19 tournament wins and netted him the War Bond equivalent of $52,511. In addition to this he had a collection of top-3 finishes that would have delighted any other player. It was no wonder that he was described by Tommy Armour as 'the finest golfer I have seen'. Even the great Bobby Jones said, 'At my best I never came close to the golf Nelson shoots.'

Golf was increasingly big business by the start of 1945. In May the WBO ban on the manufacture of golf balls was lifted, a timely relief to Byron Nelson and the rest who, according to Fred Corcoran, 'were paying up to four bucks for a pre-war pellet' – not that $4 made much of a dent in Nelson's prize money that season. Losing out to Sam Snead in the Los Angeles Open in January, Nelson hit back immediately winning the Phoenix Open with a last-round charge that saw him home in 32 for a 10-under-par total of 274. Second place finishes in the Tucson Open and Texas Open were followed by back-to-back victories in the Corpus Christi Open and the New Orleans Open with the season barely 2 months old.

Discharged from the Navy after 26 months because of a slipped disc, Snead beat Nelson in a dramatic play-off at the Gulfport Open in February to deny him 3 consecutive victories. Tied on 275, each shot 71 in the 18-hole play-off before a mistake by the Texan enabled Snead to win with par on the first extra hole. This was the start of a mini-streak for Snead, who then beat Nelson by 7 strokes to win the Pensacola Open

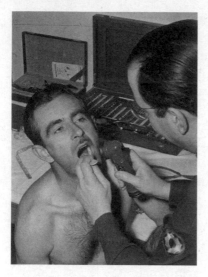

1940 Masters winner Lloyd Mangrum, subsequently decorated for his heroism in the Battle of the Bulge, sits his army medical in Los Angeles.

before picking up top prize in Jacksonville the following week. Nelson finished sixth in florida, Snead leading 4-3 in tournament wins. Nelson's critics took this as a sign that his stranglehold on golf was well and truly over. They could not have been more wrong.

Arriving at Miami Springs Golf Club the second week in March, Nelson linked up with his old friend Jug McSpaden to win the Professional Fourball event. Winning the equivalent of $1500 in War Bonds, they beat Denny Shute and Sam Byrd 8&6 in the 36-hole final. The tournament itself was unremarkable, but it will be forever remembered as the first stepping stone in the greatest winning streak in golf.

March 16-21: **Charlotte Open, Myers Park Golf Club, Charlotte, North Carolina:** Nelson beat Snead in a play-off 69-69 to 69-73.
March 23-26: **Greensboro Open, Starmount Country Club, Greensboro, North Carolina:** Nelson beat second-place Sam Byrd by 8 strokes.
March 30-April 1: **Durham Open, Hope Valley Country Club, Durham, North Carolina:** Scores in the 80s were commonplace as the players failed to negotiate the bone-hard greens. One over par for 54 holes, Nelson shot a magnificent 5-under-par final-round 65 to win.
April 5-8: **Atlanta Open, Capital City Course, Atlanta, Georgia:** Nelson breezed round the short par-69 golf course in 13 under.
June 7-10: **Montreal Open, Islemere Golf & Country Club, Montreal, Quebec, Canada:** Having shared the honours in a

36-hole medal play/match play exhibition match against Sam
Snead to find 'the world's greatest golfer' the previous week,
Nelson beat Jug McSpaden into second place by 10 strokes.

**June 14-17: Philadelphia Inquirer Invitational, Llanerch
Country Club, Philadelphia, Pennsylvania:** Runner-up for the
second week in a row, McSpaden could only watch in awe as
Nelson closed out the tournament with 7 birdies and 11 pars
for a final round of 63.

**June 29-July 1: Chicago Victory National Open, Calumet
Country Club, Chicago, Illinois:** A replacement for the still-
cancelled US Open. Nelson shot 69-68-68-70 to beat the hap-
less McSpaden and Ky Lafoon into second.

**July 9-15: PGA Championship, Moraine Country Club, Dayton,
Ohio:** Mentally exhausted and complaining of back pains,
Nelson tied with Johnny Revolta to win the 36-hole qualifying
event on 6 under par. In the match play stage, Nelson carved
his way through the strong field defeating Gene Sarazen, Mike
Turnesa, Densmore Shute, Claude Harmon en route to beating Sam Byrd 4 and 3 in the final. After playing an incredible 37
under par for 204 holes Nelson said, 'I feel like I'm a hundred
years old.'

**July 26-30: Tam O' Shanter All American Open, Tam
O' Shanter Country Club, Chicago, Illinois:** Having taken the
previous week off, Nelson achieved a 19-under-par total that
beat veteran Gene Sarazen and Lieutenant Ben Hogan into
second place. The richest event of the year: his prize for winning was $13,600.

**August 2-4: Canadian Open, Thornhill Country Club,
Toronto, Canada:** Playing on an extremely testing course with
par cut from 72 to 70, Nelson shot a 'level par' total of 280
after 4 rounds of 68-72-72-68.

The longest winning streak in golf, Nelson's 11 consecutive
victories beat the previous record of 3. Sadly the streak ended
at the Memphis Open the following week, when 29-year-old
Freddie Haas became the first amateur in over a decade to win
a top-class pro tournament. Despite finishing fourth, Nelson's
relief was obvious. While press coverage had been almost
non-existent at the start of his run, turning lukewarm around
the Montreal Open in June, it had become red-hot by the time
he teed-off in the final of the PGA Championship in July. His
attempt at 12 consecutive tournament wins would have

Ben Hogan autographs the cards that confirm he shot 5 under par to set a new course record at Fort Worth in Texas in June 1946.

received even greater coverage had it not coincided with the dramatic news that Japan had surrendered in the Pacific! Fielding question after question about how far he could go, Nelson had desperately wanted to get on with the business of playing golf; now that his winning run was ended he could do exactly that. Competing in the flamboyantly named Supreme Open at Knoxville a few days later, he raced through the field, winning by 10 from Sam Byrd in second place and by 11 over Ben Hogan in third.

Back from the Army, Hogan battled hard for the remainder of the 1945 season. In early September Nelson won at Spokane with rounds of 66-70-66-64. Hogan hit back the following week at Portland with a new record-winning total of 261 after rounds of 65-69-63-64. Barely two weeks later, Nelson bettered this at Seattle with rounds of 62-68-63-66 for a total of 259 with the closest finisher 13 strokes back!

Nelson reigned supreme, and as the season drew to a close there were still enough tournaments to turn 1945 into a victory parade. After taking a much-needed month-long break he returned to action in mid-December at the Fort Worth Open in Texas, played at Glen Garden, the course where he and Hogan had caddied as youngsters. Nelson was involved in a car accident en route to the course but it had little effect on his game. finishing with closing rounds of 66-70, his 273 total was enough to record his 18th win of the year in PGA-sanctioned events.

Nelson was voted 'Athlete of the Year' for the second consecutive year by the writers of the Associated Press, and his
season was a miracle of consistency. Winning money in every
event he entered, he never missed a cut and bettered his previous stroke average by over a stroke per round at 68.33. Even
in the days of Hagen and Jones, golf had never witnessed such
consistently low scoring and while critics would carp about
the quality of tournament venues and lack of quality competition, his record is not easily dismissed.

While it is true that many of his scores were made on
courses lacking the length of Baltusrol, the punishing rough
of Oakmont and the lightning-fast greens of Interlachen, the
conditions were the same for everyone. As for lack of competition, the only significant player missing throughout the 1945
season was Lloyd Mangrum, who was still recovering from his
wartime injuries. Sam Snead, discharged from the Navy at the
end of 1944, played in all but a handful of events in 1945 until
a freak baseball injury sidelined him for the last 3 events of
Nelson's streak. Ben Hogan compiled some of the lowest
scores of his career, winning 5 out of 19 events played after
rejoining the tour in August. As for the so-called also-rans,
they included proven tournament winners like McSpaden,
Byrd, Hines, Shute and Turnesa along with vibrant new talent
like Frank Stranahan and Cary Middlecoff.

Nelson was simply too good for all of them, and had been
responsible for over $1 million worth of War Bond sales. He
was hailed as the greatest American golfer since Bobby Jones.
Benefiting from this interest, his tournament pro's could barely believe their luck as the news came through that Fred
Corcoran was demanding a minimum of $10,000 in prize
money *no matter what the event* in 1946. (With backers queuing
up to throw money at the game, the innovative director of the
PGA Tournament Division even considered having one set of
sponsors for the even years and another for the odd!)

Nelson and the rest were now able to play 37 weeks out of
52. Competing for over $400,000 in official prize money,

American professionals began cashing in on golf's popularity. In 1946 Johnny Bulla, a registered pilot, began ferrying his fellow Tour pro's around in a plane he had bought the previous December, and was never short of paying passengers. The insurance cost of transporting players like Hogan, Snead and Nelson would make such a scheme unthinkable today.

Prize money statistics were secondary for American golf fans. All they wanted to know was: who was the number one golfer in the world? Recognising the opportunity to raise the game's profile even higher, Fred Corcoran built up the 'hated-rivals' angle between Nelson and Hogan in off-the-record briefings with the golfing press. Remarkably, it was not too far from the truth. Before the war they had been as friendly as two hard-edged, uncommunicative, battle-until-you-drop Texans constantly pitted against one another could possibly be. In 1937, for example, Nelson had supplied Hogan with the driver that had transformed his game. But by 1946 their relationship had frosted to the point where they barely spoke. It was said that Hogan resented Nelson's wartime triumphs and made no secret of his intention to win back the number one position he had last held in 1942. As for Nelson, he wanted to carry on winning tournaments no matter who was in the field.

As the 1946 season got under way, the suspense mounted.

Picking up where he had left off the previous year, Nelson began by winning in Los Angeles and San Francisco with Hogan finishing 5 and 10 strokes back respectively. Hitting another rich vein of form in summer, Nelson won both the Columbus Invitational and Chicago Victory Open. Hogan in reply won the St Petersburg Open and the Miami Fourball (with Jimmy Demaret) before recording successive victories in the Colonial Invitation, Western Open and Goodhall Round Robin Tournament. Yet it was fast turning into a bittersweet year for Hogan. In April, he lost in a play-off

Nelson and Hogan waiting to tee off in the play-off for the 1942 Masters.

to Herman Keiser at the Masters. Then in June he missed a 5-foot putt on the final green at Canterbury that would have taken him into a US Open play-off with Vic Ghezzi, Lloyd Mangrum and Byron Nelson. With Hogan desperate to win his first major, Nelson narrowly missed winning his sixth, losing to Mangrum in a tight play-off.

It was honours even in the weeks leading up to the 1946 PGA Championship at Portland, Oregon. By the start of August Hogan had won more money than Nelson but Byron had played fewer tournaments and had a better stroke average. Then came a bombshell no one expected – citing increasing back problems, Byron Nelson announced that, at the age of 34, he intended to retire and the PGA would be his farewell appearance. The weekly grind of travelling back and forth across the country, giving countless interviews, had become too much for this intensely private man. After the tournament he would head back to his 1500-acre farm in Roanoke, Texas, only returning for the 1947 Ryder Cup and the Masters each spring. (His old sparring partner Jug McSpaden would play one more season before retiring with a total of 17 career victories to his name.)

Understandably, the PGA Championship attracted a huge amount of interest with everyone wanting a valedictory final between Nelson and Hogan. But it was not to be. Playing in different halves of the draw, Ben made it to the final where Ed 'Porky' Oliver, who had defeated Nelson in the quarter-final, was waiting for him. Thirty-six holes later Hogan beat Oliver by 6&4 and was crowned undisputed world number one. As he held the Wanamaker trophy aloft, maybe it crossed his mind that the only player who could reasonably expect to challenge his dominance over the next few years was currently driving back to his ranch in distant Texas. As one golf journalist wrote, 'With World War II a fast receding memory the Hogan era has just begun...'

The memory of World War II might indeed be fading fast, but the days of golf played within reach of the battlefield were not yet over.

Fred Corcoran, Tournament Director of the United States PGA during the later years of World War II, once declared wartime golf 'rather pointless'.

With rumours persisting about golf balls that could fly over 300 yards, the USGA developed a machine in 1941 to test the velocity of a golf ball at impact. Plans for limiting initial velocity were put on hold until after the war.

In 1942 the United States Golf Association urged all Army Camps to install a driving range or practice putting green.

CHAPTER XV

Back to the Future:
Korea, Vietnam and 9-11:
1946 to modern times

FROM KOREA TO KABUL, regional conflicts, border disputes and terrorist incidents have littered the pages of history over the past 50 years. And golf, as ever, continues to be played within earshot of the fighting.

From the late 1940s onward, golf grew in popularity as the direct result of many American soldiers, sailors and airmen being introduced to the sport during their service years – including former Green Beret Earl Woods, father of Tiger. In 1953, when Eisenhower became President, just over 3 million Americans played golf. By 1961 that figure had doubled, and there was no class division: congressman or concierge, golf was considered 'a game for all'. Wherever American servicemen went, their clubs inevitably followed. (Even 'Ike' himself learned to play golf while attending the

General Dwight D. Eisenhower plays off the road on the famous 17th 'Road Hole' at St Andrews in October 1946.

*An attack helicopter obstructs the green for Donald Sutherland
and Elliot Gould in M*A*S*H.*

Army's Command and General Staff School at Fort
Leavenworth in Kansas in 1925.)

The Korean War from 1950 to 1953 was the first major
conflict after World War II, and for many servicemen golf was
an invaluable reminder of home in this most inhospitable of
countries. The image of actors Donald Sutherland (as
Hawkeye Pierce) and Elliot Gould (Trapper John McIntyre)
hitting golf balls off a rock-strewn helicopter pad in the movie
M*A*S*H was probably not far from the truth.

After Korea came Vietnam. What started as a small US
assistance programme to help train South Vietnamese troops
against the Communist-backed Viet Cong guerrillas grew
into a massive military and naval campaign. Once more US
troops found themselves in action against an elusive enemy,
and between 1961 and 1973 almost 60,000 American lives were
lost.

Public backing for the campaign was solid at first, but as

Bob Hope entertains the crew of the aircraft carrier USS Ticonderoga
during the Vietnam War in December 1965.

casualties mounted from 1965 onward, the tide began to turn.
President Lyndon Johnson gave up golf completely, saying
that the American people would 'eat me alive' if they heard
that he was playing golf while US servicemen were dying

overseas. Then, as the pressure became intolerable and his health began to falter, he announced in June 1967 that he was giving up alcohol and taking up his clubs once more. Describing this decision as 'alarming', James Reston, a columnist for the *New York Times*, wrote that substituting golf for whiskey was 'the worst miscalculation since the start of the Vietnam War. Golf is not an escape from anything. It is itself an agony.'

Following in the footsteps of Bob Hope and Bing Crosby in World War II, reigning US Open champion Billy Casper made a morale-boosting visit to combat troops in 1966. Allergic to the sprays used on the greens during the Florida section of the PGA Tour, he was invited to play in the Philippines Open and immediately contacted the Department of Defense about staging a series of front-line golf clinics. With public attitudes already hardening after 5 years of war, his offer was taken up and his 16-day trip received enormous coverage in the golfing press. He was accompanied by Hack Miller, a sports journalist from Salt Lake City,

Having given a golf clinic on the hangar deck of aircraft carriers *Enterprise* and *Yorktown* en route to the combat zone, Casper took his travelling golf show to some of the more remote jungle outposts, known as 'far-forward' camps. He was dropped in by helicopter in a blaze of noise and whirling sand. Contrasting with the khaki-clad GIs, he always dressed in brightly coloured golfing attire and must have made a tempting target for any Viet Cong sniper as he sprinted headlong towards the safety of the perimeter fence clutching an armful of golf clubs! Spending time visiting the wounded and chatting about sport with the battle-weary soldiers, he offered a quick lesson to anyone who wanted one, before smashing a few drives into the jungle. With 'Charley' (the Viet Cong) an ever-present danger, no one could accuse Billy Casper of not 'doing his bit' for the war effort.

The American star recalled one particular visit to a Special Forces camp:

Billy Casper gives a golfing class to GIs in Vietnam.

*It seemed incongruous that these men, concerned daily
with self-preservation, should be interested in me, or in
golf... We talked about sports in general and golf in
particular, and then I asked if they would like a lesson in
golf? They said, 'Sure!' So with a soda pop can as a golf
ball I gave them a 15-minute clinic. They wanted to know
about my diet, Arnie Palmer's comeback, why Jack
Nicklaus missed the first part of the tour? They asked
about new rules, money, and PGA affairs. Then the
captain suggested maybe, we had better leave before the VC
had time to zero in on us with their long-range weapons. I
hated to leave these men. It was the first time in my adult
life that I wanted to pick up a shovel and help. Leaving
them was like saying good-bye to friends who were in need.*

It made me feel a little like a coward – but there was another camp waiting...

In what amounted to a whistle-stop tour of Vietnam, Casper gave exhibitions at Subic Bay and Clark Field along with visits to DeNang, Pleiku and Dalat. Giving away over 400 golf balls, he delighted the watching audiences by smashing hundreds more into minefields and 'Charley'-held territory. Targeting rice paddies and even a cemetery, he nearly caused a diplomatic incident after a Vietnamese funeral crossed his driving line. He was shot at by the Viet Cong while transferring from land to sea, and a beach on the South China Sea was swept for mines shortly before he gave a clinic on sand play! The gregarious star was deeply affected by the brutality of war. Barely hours before he arrived at one camp a young lieutenant had stepped on a mine and lost his leg. Casper recalled: 'I wondered right then, what business a golfer had in this place?'

As in every war, much of that 'business' was propaganda value. Public opinion back in the USA was paramount and while serviceman no doubt welcomed high-profile visits by stars of stage, screen and golf, it was the positive message brought home by these celebrities that really counted. As the patriotic Billy Casper explained in *Golf Digest*:

On the eve of the final day singles at the 1999 Ryder Cup match at Brookline, Massachusetts, the American team was trailing Europe 10-6 and facing a second straight defeat on home soil. Captain Ben Crenshaw asked his close friend George W. Bush to help boost the team's battered morale. The then Governor of Texas began by reading the letter from Colonel William Travis to the American people on the eve of the Battle of the Alamo in 1836. Leading a rag-tag collection of brave Texans against the might of Santa Anna's Mexican Army, Travis described how 'Our flag still proudly waves from the wall. I shall never surrender nor retreat', before declaring it was 'Victory or death' for his brave band of brothers. The effect that Saturday evening was electric. David Duval was among those visibly moved by the speech, and the following day he was instrumental in turning certain American defeat into a narrow 14-13 win.

I found the morale of the men to be extremely high – never a complaint. Always a desire to get Charley. My own morale really was bolstered, especially after seeing the spirit of the wounded in the hospitals. That's when I realised that what we are fighting for is really worthwhile. One man at DeNang had lost both legs at the knees. 'I'll be all right as soon as they get me some equipment down there,' he said, pointing to where his feet had been. 'I can still make a living and I may find a little time to play golf.' He asked me if I would teach him. I promised him that I would go to wherever he was and help him learn to play again. Our escort officer, Lt. Mike Griffin from Lewiston, Idaho, was one of these spirited men. Mike had been shot three times – once with a hard blast in the midriff. Yet, he was anxious to get back to his unit. He figured that there were a lot of Charleys in War Zone D that he and his outfit hadn't found.

By Christmas 1972 the mood of the country was split, with many Americans keen to see an immediate end to the decade-long war. Johnson's successor as president, Richard Nixon, decided that he needed to sound out opinion further afield than Washington. His old golfing buddies Arnold Palmer and Bob Hope were summoned to his private home in San Clemente, California, the following February, to give their thoughts on the 'Vietnam problem'. Nixon desperately wanted an end to the conflict and, typically, Arnie advised the President to 'go for the green' in any decision he had to take.

Appreciative of his support, Nixon turned down the chance to play golf that weekend even with Arnie as his house guest. Indeed he was reluctant to play golf at any time during

During the Falklands War, Max Hastings, who was reporting the war for the London *Evening Standard*, described the final push into the capital Port Stanley as 'like liberating a suburban golf club'.

the conflict – a view with which Palmer had the utmost sympathy, as he explained in his autobiography *A Golfer's Life*:

> *With thousands of young American men and women dying in Vietnam and the college campuses of this country exploding with antiwar demonstrations, it probably wouldn't have sat well with the parents of those young people to know the Commander-in-Chief had taken the afternoon off to beat the ball around Congressional or Burning Tree.*

Later the same year Nixon ordered American troops out of Vietnam. Now all he had to worry about was a little scandal called Watergate...

No international sporting event was as profoundly affected by the events of 11 September 2001 as the Ryder Cup. As the shell-shocked western world struggled to come to terms with the terrorist attack on mainland America, the PGA of America and Europe had to decide whether the biannual

A friendly round at the rather rough-looking Kabul Golf Club after
the liberation of Afghanistan in 2001. This tournament was staged by
golf-hungry war correspondents, and the old man hitting a chip was
former caddie Mohammed Nazin, who had also tended the bullet-scarred
9-hole course prior to the Russian invasion in 1986. Not long after this
competition took place, the ruling Taliban regime declared golf
un-Islamic and the course fell into disrepair. Would visiting golfers have
infringed the 14-club rule by carrying a rifle over their shoulder?

match scheduled for September 28-30 at the Belfry should be
cancelled or not. Opinion was understandably split. There
were those who said, 'Golf must not give way to the terror-
ists,' while others believed that playing golf so soon after the
World Trade Center tragedy would be utterly immoral.

Then came the question of who would be in the teams if
the match were postponed for a year, or for 2 years. Media
speculation was endless. Europe and the USA both had out-of-
form players, and if the qualification process were to be
extended or amended, both teams would change significantly.

The Iraq War, 2003.
Top On an improvised golf
course in the desert of western
Kuwait US Army Staff Sergeant
Bryce Ivings chips to the hole
using the pitching wedge his
parents sent him from home in
Florida. Bottom US Army
soldiers Jeff McFarland and
Chad Pringle line up a putt on
the 3rd hole.

Given extra time, Justin Leonard, hero of the 1999 victory at The Country Club in Brookline, might have played his way onto the American team along with the talented Chris DiMarco. And if American team captain Curtis Strange had been given more time to ponder his wild-card picks, Paul Azinger – suffering as he was with back problems – might no longer have been his top choice. As for Europe, Ian Poulter and possibly Justin Rose might have ousted struggling Welshman Phillip Price or even the injury-threatened Lee Westwood. The permutations seemed never-ending.

It came as a relief when the decision was finally made to postpone the match for 12 months with both teams remaining the same. In the end it proved to be the right choice. Retaining much of the patriotism and competitive fire of previous matches, the 34th Ryder Cup was eventually played on 27-29 September 2002. In the pre-match build-up, the *Daily Telegraph* summed up the feelings of many: 'Let's say this at full volume, there is no link between the Ryder Cup or any golf tournament and Sept. 11th.'

They were wrong. The 'lost' Ryder Cup match of 2001 will be forever linked with the events of that terrible autumn day. and the attitude of both teams reflected that. Solemn and respectful, the opening ceremony acknowledged the victims of 9-11 while looking forward to the future. Calling upon the spirit of comradeship that was the very bedrock of the Ryder Cup, Strange gestured towards the national flags – including, of course, the Stars and Stripes – that flew overhead. Reminding everyone what a truly global game golf had become over the past five centuries he said, 'Every country represented here lost citizens that day.'

Speaking to the press shortly afterwards, European captain Sam Torrance commented, 'I don't think we will ever forget why the matches were postponed but I've always said once the tee goes in the ground Friday morning, we're going to have a competitive match in the best traditions of the game. That is what makes golf special.'

No one disagreed, and both teams performed brilliantly, with the result in the balance right up to the very end. As so many times before, golf had faced adversity and come through with flying colours.

BIBLIOGRAPHY

Behrend, John. *John Ball of Hoylake*. Grant Books, Worcestershire, 1989.

Braid, James. *Advanced Golf*. Methuen, London, 1908.

Browning, Robert K. *A History of Golf*. J. M. Dent, London, 1955.

Campbell, Patrick. *How to Become a Scratch Golfer*. Anthony Blond, London, 1963.

Clark, Robert. *Golf: A Royal & Ancient Game*. Edinburgh, 1875.

Cooper, Artemis. *Cairo in the War*. Penguin, London, 1995.

Dalconen, A.J. *Golf: The History of the Royal & Ancient Game*. Salamander, London, 1995.

Darwin, Bernard. *Golf between the Wars*. 1944.

Darwin, Bernard. *James Braid*. 1952.

Fitzpatrick. H.L. *Golf Don'ts*. Doubleday-Page, 1900.

Golf Digest.

Golf Monthly, IPC Publications, Stamford Street, London SE1.

Golfing Magazine; ed. George Philpott.

Golf Illustrated/Golf Weekly. EMAP Active, Peterborough.

Harris, Robert. *Sixty Years of Golf*. Batchworth Press, 1953.

Hutchinson, Horace et al. *Golf: Longmans Green*, London, 1890.

Hutchinson, Horace. *Fifty Years of Golf*. Country Life, London, 1919.

Keeler, O. B. *The Bobby Jones Story*. Tupper and Love, Atlanta, GA, 1959.

Kenneth R. *The Mental Side of Golf: A Study of the Game*. Muller, London, 1955.

Kerr. J. *The Golf Book of East Lothian*. Constable, Edinburgh, 1896.

Longhurst, Henry. Articles in the *Daily Telegraph*, London.

Mappin, Major G. F. *The Golfing You*. Skeffington, 1948.

Nisbet's *Golf Year Book*. *Golf Illustrated*, 1914.

Ouimet, Francis. The Francis Ouimet Scholarship Fund, Inc., Weston, MA.

Palmer, Arnold, *A Golfer's Life*, Random House, New York, 2000.

Park, William. *The Game of Golf*, Longman, London, 1899.

Price, Charles, ed. *The American Golfer* magazine.

Rice, Grantland. *The American Golfer* magazine.

Robertson, James K. *St.Andrews*. Citizen Office, Fife, Scotland, 1967.

Sassoon, Siegfried. *The Complete Memoirs of George Sherston*. Faber & Faber, London, 1937.

Simpson, Sir Walter. *The Art of Golf*, Hamilton, Edinburgh, 1887.

Sneddon, Richard. *The Golf Stream*, Dorrance, Philadelphia, 1941.

Veteran, A. *The Secret of Golf for Occasional Players*. Methuen, London, 1922.

Wind, Herbert W. *The Story of American Golf*. Farrar, Straus, New York, 1948.

Wind, Herbert W. *The Complete Golfer*. Simon and Schuster, New York, 1954.